ODGERS - 1951

LARRY KING
Why I Love Baseball

with **Julie McCarron**
edited by **Michael Viner**

New Millennium Press

First published in the United States of America in 2004
by New Millennium Entertainment, Inc.
301 N. Canon Drive #214
Beverly Hills, CA 90210
www.NewMillenniumPress.com

Library of Congress Cataloging-in-Publication Data
available upon request.
ISBN: 1-932407-10-3

Jacket design by
Interior design by Carolyn Wendt

Printed in the United States of America

10 9 8 7 6 5 4 3 2 1

In all our lives there are hits, strikeouts, and the occasional home run.
This book is dedicated to my two young sons,
Chance King and his brother Cannon King,
two of the cherished home runs of my life.

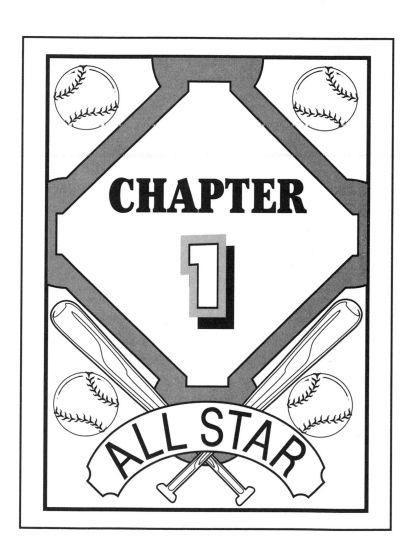

CHAPTER

1

ALL STAR

October 3, 1951 was the saddest day of my life. On that afternoon at the Polo Grounds in New York City, Bobby Thomson hit the shot that was heard 'round the world. He homered off Ralph Branca in the bottom of the ninth inning, producing a 5–4 Giants' victory over my beloved Dodgers in the final game of the three-game playoff to determine the winner of the National League pennant. It is the only time in my life that I seriously contemplated suicide. I thought of maybe going to the Brooklyn Bridge, but I figured the line would be too long.

I was approaching my eighteenth birthday, and by that time the Dodgers were part of my neurological system. They had been ahead by thirteen games in the pennant race in the middle of August that year, and seemed a lock to go to the World Series. But the Giants—the hated New York Giants—kept coming and coming. We'd win two out of three; they'd win three out of three. It seemed they couldn't lose. They were managed by the once beloved and now hated (at least by true Dodger fans) Leo Durocher, the former skipper of the Dodgers who had been fired in July of the 1948 season only to be immediately hired by the Giants.

But in 1951 the teams ended the season in a tie. In fact, we had to sweat it out to get the tie. The Giants had won on the last Sunday of the season early and easy. We had to go into extra innings to beat the docile Phillies in Philadelphia, saved by a great catch and a home run from Jackie Robinson. We lost the first game of the three-game playoff at Ebbets Field 3–1. Thomson homered in that game too. We won the second game at the Polo Grounds 10–0, and seemed invincible. And then, and then . . . October 3, 1951.

We led 4–1 going into the bottom of the ninth. The Giants came at us, got to 4–2, then with runners on first and third and one out, the Scotsman, as Thomson was called, delivered the potent blow.

Truth be told, I really shouldn't have been a Dodger fan at all. My father loved the Yankees. He was a Russian immigrant who loved all sports, but especially the Yankees. I remember as a little kid listening to Yankee games on the radio and hearing my father talk about Gehrig, Ruth, and DiMaggio. Then, as I started to take an interest in baseball, my father suddenly died. I was nine-and-a-half years old. I was both devastated and angry. In retrospect, I think I took his death as an abandonment. I was mad at him for leaving me. I refused to go to the funeral. I lost interest in school. We moved from one neighborhood in Brooklyn to another. I couldn't be a Yankee fan; it was too close to my hurt feelings. So I switched my allegiance to the beloved "Bums" of Flatbush, the Dodgers.

My father had died in June. That August my cousin Bernie took me to my first big league game. I remember it like it was yesterday. Up until that time, all I had to go on was Red Barber's voice describing Dodger baseball on the radio. He was a master of technique. In fact, I think I learned the game from him.

It was a clear, sunny day. I remember walking into Ebbets Field and seeing that magnificent old stadium, smelling the popcorn and the beer and the hot dogs, seeing the brown dirt against the green grass and the crisp, white uniforms of the Dodgers (their color is still the whitest in all of baseball). They were playing the Cincinnati Reds, who wore their visiting gray. Curt Davis was pitching for the Dodgers. We won, I think the score was 4–3 or 5–4. I can still vividly recall how my heart pounded just at seeing a major league field. By the way, that feeling remains to this day. I've been to hundreds and hundreds of games, and every time I walk into a ballpark I get the same feeling I had at my first game, that summer day in 1943.

I was too poor to buy tickets to many games. We were on relief because of my father's death. (Relief was what we now call welfare.) It meant that the City of New York provided for our rent and other necessities of life. Indeed, it was the City of New York that bought me my first pair of glasses. But I could listen to the games, follow "dem bums" as they were called, day in and day out on the radio. Occasionally the Police Athletic League would take a bunch of us to a game for free. We'd sit in the upper left-field stands and root, root, root for the home team. Sometimes we even went to see the hated Yankees play.

My best friend, a rather brash kid named Herbie Cohen, who remains my best friend to this day, was one of the Yankee fans in our neighborhood. I still hate him for that. (By the way, Herbie went on to become the best-selling author of the classic business bible *You Can Negotiate Anything* and an advisor to U.S. Presidents and heads of state. But sixty years ago he was just another Brooklyn kid, and a true-blue Yankee fan.) Anyway, this one summer afternoon, we must have been about ten or eleven years old, a bunch of us kids got taken into the outfield at Yankee Stadium for a baseball clinic. Billy Pierce, the White Sox pitcher, was conducting the clinic. As he demonstrated how to hold the ball to throw a curve, Herbie yelled, "Wrong!" Billy was shocked, needless to say, and so were the rest of us. But Billy asked Herbie his name, and after Herbie explained the "right" way to throw a curve, Billy replied, "Well kid, you're right, but I hold it this way. Most pitchers hold it the way you suggested." Herbie looked at us with that pompous air. And I wanted to kill him. Naturally the Yankees won that day, because the Yankees always won.

When we could afford to go to games we would sit in the bleachers. The price was fifty cents a ticket. We'd invariably get there early to watch batting practice. And as far as I'm concerned, batting practice and infield practice are as much a part of the game of baseball as the game itself. It's a ritual that goes back to when baseball started in the nineteenth century. The true fan always gets there early. That remains the case for me to this day. I never walk in just in time for the first pitch. I want to see batting practice, I want to see the players lingering around the batting cage. My status in the media now allows me to go on the field and stand around that cage. It is one of the great thrills of my life to mingle with major league baseball players and talk about the game I love.

One thing is for sure, baseball was full of characters in the forties and fifties—so many people who were larger than the game. My favorite ballplayer as a kid was Billy Cox, third baseman for the Dodgers. We acquired him from the Pirates in one of the great trades of all time. We also got Preacher Roe. Cox had suffered from malaria in World War II and was always very sullen looking, but, God, could he play third base. He would hold his glove in his right hand while the pitch was coming to the plate, gently slide it onto the left hand as the batter swung, catch the ball, sometimes look at the ball as if to read the imprint, then fire to first for the out.

I pretended to be Billy Cox when I played softball. I would try to hold the glove in my right hand and slip it onto the left. I'd try to walk like him, try to bat like him. Sometimes it looked like he would jump to hit a pitch. But he was the best, just the best.

I remember Brooks Robinson, the legendary Orioles' third baseman, telling me once how Casey Stengel, then the Mets' manager, had told him before an exhibition game in Miami that Brooks was the second-best third baseman that he, Stengel, had ever seen. Who was the best? Brooks inquired. And Stengel said, "Number 3 from Brooklyn." Stengel forgot names easily. Adding, "And he had a better arm."

The Dodger first baseman was Gil Hodges. I saw his wife not too long ago, at the opening game of the Brooklyn Cyclones, a Class-A minor league team owned by the Mets. They play at a brand-new minor league ballpark about ten minutes away from where I grew up. His widow and I talked about Gil, the kind of person he was, and how suddenly he left us. Gil Hodges was in a long slump once, and priests in Brooklyn had prayers said for him in all of the parishes. It was that kind of place, Brooklyn.

Jackie Robinson anchored second and the wonderful Pee Wee Reese played shortstop. I got to know Pee Wee rather well. The story of his connection with Jackie is larger than the sport and only adds to my love for it. They are currently building a statue of Reese and Robinson to be erected near that new ballpark in Brooklyn. It's a great idea. Pee Wee (he got that nickname from being a marbles champion) came from Kentucky, and had never played with or against a black athlete. When Jackie joined the Dodgers, Pee Wee knew that a lot of people back home in Louisville didn't want him to play with Robinson. Pee Wee not only played with him, he became one of his best friends. Once, in Chicago, there was a threat made on Robinson's life. The FBI posted men throughout Wrigley Field. Reese went over to Robinson and said, "I've got an idea, Jackie. Why don't we all wear number 42, and then they won't know who to shoot."

When Robinson broke the color line at hotels by refusing to get off a bus in St. Louis and go to the Negroes' hotel, but went with the rest of his teammates to the Chase Hotel, which had never housed a black, Reese, the captain of the Dodgers, said to the clerk, "You take Robinson or you take none of us." Robinson stayed at the Chase. Years later, when I asked Pee Wee how he was able to throw aside his upbringing, he said simply, "He was my teammate."

The catcher on that Dodger team of my youth was Roy Campanella, another young black athlete who excelled at the game, until a tragic winter accident in an automobile left him wheelchair-bound for the rest of his life. Campy had a much different temperament than Robinson; he was effusive, always smiling, hated making trouble and argued with Robinson over his orneriness. Needless to say, watching Campy play was a sight to behold.

Our left fielder was Gene Hermanski, then later Andy Pafko. Left field was always a problem in Brooklyn. Our center fielder was Duke Snider. Snider was moody, but a wonderful athlete. Our right fielder was Carl Furillo, he of the magic arm and the steadiness of a .299 hitter. I loved that team. I loved the pitchers, Roe and Newcombe, and the incredible Carl Erskine, and Branca, and all the rest. I remember Erskine telling me once what it was like to stand on the mound in Ebbets Field, holding a ball in his hand, about to make the first pitch of the game, and think to himself, "'How blessed I am. I'm a major league pitcher in this historic ballpark, pitching for this crazy, terrific team. Little Carl Erskine from Indiana is a Dodger.' I was so proud."

Think about this: living at the same time, playing center field in the city of New York, were Mickey Mantle, Willie Mays, and Duke Snider. For the Yankees, Giants, and Dodgers, respectively. Terry Cashman wrote a great song about that called "Talkin' Baseball (Willie, Mickey And The Duke)". It was all about talking baseball, something, by the way, I still do almost every day.

Today we gather at Nate 'N Al's Deli in Beverly Hills to talk baseball. Poets have written of this feeling much better than I. Baseball is a magical game. Owners and players and critics can hurt it a lot, off the field. But on the field, nothing can damage it. It's really a kind of genius game. Whoever invented it, whether it was Abner Doubleday or Alfred Spaulding or Abraham Lincoln, as some people think, it is perfection. Just think, what if the bases were a little longer than ninety feet apart, or a little shorter? What if the pitcher's mound were a little further back, or a little closer in? It would be a whole different, terrible game. But that is not the case.

Besides the warm memories from my childhood, there are a million reasons why I love baseball. I love the crowd. It's the only game where you can continually talk to whomever is sitting next to you and completely observe everything going on at the same time. It's the only game where you can constantly relive the events therein. And it's a game that keeps throwing its own curve balls. Whenever I go to a baseball game, it seems I see things I've never seen before. The ball that goes into the stands, hits the railing and lands on someone's head . . . the umpires wearing civilian clothes because their uniforms failed to arrive with their airplane. . . .

And even food tastes better at ballparks. A hot dog at a game, steamed or grilled, just tastes better. Why is that? Is it just the atmosphere? I think that everything at a ball game is a little brighter, a little sharper, a little bit more in focus. It's a magical break from the worries and cares of everyday life. Simply put, there's nothing about it I don't love.

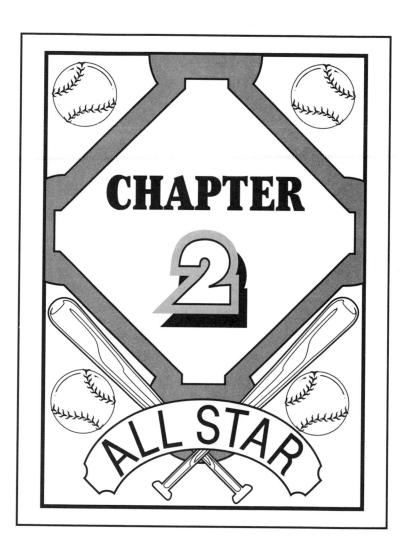

CHAPTER

2

ALL STAR

At this point, readers, it should be emphasized that I am no longer a Dodgers' fan. They left Brooklyn in 1957 to move west, and when they moved, they moved out of my heart. The Dodgers belonged in Brooklyn. They still do in my opinion. I could never develop the same feeling for the Los Angeles Dodgers, even though Sandy Koufax went to the same high school as I did, and Tommy Lasorda is a friend, and I know and like many of the players. I just can't root for the team that deserted the borough that loved them so much.

That same year, I went down to Miami to break into broadcasting. Miami was where the Orioles trained in the spring, so I became a Baltimore fan, and sort of watched them grow and rooted for them throughout the season. There was no major league baseball then in Miami. They had a Triple-A team, then a Single-A team. I never thought major league baseball would come to south Florida. When I moved to Washington in 1978, the Orioles were also the closest team to where I lived. So I remain a supporter to this day. I sat next to the late

Edward Bennett Williams and the columnist George Will when the Orioles won the 1983 World Series, defeating the Phillies in five games. When the final out was made, the joy that went through me is indescribable. I watched Mr. Williams, probably America's most famous and best criminal attorney, and owner of the team, go out of his mind with joy over winning a baseball game.

I also have a strong interest in the doings of the New York Mets. Freddie Wilpon, their owner, and I went to school together in Brooklyn. And the Mets feel to me the most like the old-time Dodgers in the way they play, the spirit of the team, and the feelings they evoke in the fans. My ultimate wish would be a Mets/Orioles World Series that never ends. The seventh game would be called by snow with the teams tied in the ninth inning, and the snowstorm would last till December, and baseball would declare both teams champions.

Come to think of it, baseball is a game that's full of idiosyncracies. Why, for instance, four balls and three strikes? Why not four and four, or three and three? You can't really succeed as a hitter. No one has ever hit .500, meaning, as Ted Williams once said, "I failed to do what I was paid to do, six and a half out of every ten times I came to bat." How do you take a round bat and hit a round ball straight ahead? How do you hit at all with a man sitting behind you signaling what to throw to a man sixty feet, six inches away, who will fire it at you at ninety plus miles an hour while seven other people are trolling the field, ready to catch whatever you hit? How in the world do they do it? How do they hit it over the outfielders, or between them?

And you're on your own when you step to the plate. But if you're a good hitter, you will make it, no matter where you are, what your living condition is, where you grew up—because you are not dependent on others. You could be a good quarterback in high school and have lousy wide receivers. A good basketball player is not noticed until someone throws him the ball. You could be a good hockey player with no one to get you the puck. Ah, but if you can hit a baseball . . . that will get you a try-out with a major league team, and you can be on that team. It does not require politics. If you can do it, you will do it. There is no great player living on a farm in Montana.

Another thing I love about baseball is that it has no clock. When I say I'm going to the game, I cannot tell you when I'll be back. Every other game has a definitive end time. Baseball does not. Lovers don't like end times. I'm getting a bit wistful here. I remember when the Boston Red Sox defeated the Tampa Bay Devil Rays in the first game of a doubleheader 22–4. In the second game the Red Sox led the hapless Devil Rays 4–0 in the ninth inning at Boston, and lost 5–4. If it were a football game with the score 28–0, and, say, eight minutes left in the fourth quarter, you could just go home. But in baseball, as long as you have an at-bat, you have a chance. As Yogi said, it ain't over till it's over.

As any baseball fan knows, the slowness of the game is part of its great charm. In fact, it's only non-fans who complain that baseball is a slow game in the first place. I wouldn't want to speed it up at all. I love its pace and its rhythm. Who wants to spend an hour and a half at a ball game? That's crazy. Two hours forty-five minutes is fine by me. Extra innings are fine by me. Double headers are swell. I can't get enough.

Beyond the game itself, it's the little things about baseball that resonate with me. I like the dugouts, where they talk about the game all throughout the game. I like the bullpen, where the relief pitchers congregate and observe, and wonder when and if they will get in. I like to watch the way outfielders move, depending on who's coming up to bat. I like the way infielders talk to each other while holding their gloves in front of their mouths. I like conferences at the mound. I love arguments, when managers come storming out, throw some dirt.

I have some great manager stories. The aforementioned Leo Durocher was one of my favorites as a kid when he managed the Dodgers. He wore number 2, so I wore number 2. I wasn't a good athlete, but I thought I could have been a manager. I still think I could be a manager. Anyway, I loved Leo, before he went over to the Giants. He was one of my heroes. Now, I'm at my first job in Miami, my first job as a broadcaster. I've been on the job about a year, it's the spring of 1958, and the Dodgers are going to come down to Miami to play the Orioles. They were now the Los Angeles Dodgers, of course, and Leo Durocher was their third-base coach.

The sports director at my radio station said, "Do you want to go and interview someone today before the game?" I said, "Oh, boy, would I love to talk to Leo Durocher, my hero." So I knew the Dodgers were still up in Vero Beach in the morning—they would fly down later that afternoon. So I placed a call to Leo; he doesn't know me, I don't know him. He was out at the moment, I leave a message to call Larry King. I go on the air, get off the air and there's a message waiting for me. Leo Durocher returned my call. What a thrill—I saved that message slip for twenty years, just to look at it. I then call him back and miss him, he calls me back and misses me—we do this five times, I have five messages from Durocher. Finally, they get on the plane and fly to Miami.

Though I'd never made contact with him, I took my tape recorder and went out to the stadium. Leo was standing at home plate hitting ground balls. There were about three thousand people in the stands. It was about an hour before the game.

I trudged toward home plate and there he stood, my hero, Leo Durocher. The man I'd called five times and missed every time, who'd returned all my calls and missed me. My hero. I approached him and said, "Mr. Durocher?" And he said, "What do you want, kid?" And I said, "I'm Larry King." And he said, screaming, "What the FUCK do you want?" Everyone in the ballpark heard it. I must have jumped back ten feet. Then he really started screaming. "Who the hell are you? Why am I calling you back? Why are you calling me?" Oh, my gosh. I was never so embarrassed and chagrined, but that was Leo. He said, "Your name sounds like someone I should know. But I don't know you." Finally I calmed him down, and he proceeded to come to the dugout and sit for an interview.

In later years, just before he died, I interviewed him on my national radio show in Washington. I had a great couple of hours with a legend, who definitely belongs in the Hall of Fame.

Casey Stengel, before he became famous as the Yankee manager, was laughed at when he managed the then Boston Braves and Dodgers in New York. The teams were never good and Casey was always kind of a clown. He came up to home plate one day to bring the lineups to the umpires, lifted his cap, and a bird flew out. When he went on to manage the Mets, his first pick in the draft choice was Hobie Landrith, a nondescript catcher. When asked why he picked a catcher as his number-one draft pick, he said, "If you don't have a catcher, you have a lot of dropped balls. There's nobody behind the plate there."

Casey once testified when Congress held antitrust hearings on the sport of baseball. He followed the Commissioner, who gave long, eloquent answers to deeply philosophical questions. When it was his turn, Casey sat down and said, "Whatever he said, goes for me double."

As anyone who knows baseball knows, Casey could talk forever. I was working in Miami, but went up to New York for the opening of the New York World's Fair in 1964. Casey was managing the New York Mets at the time, and my engineer and I went to Shea Stadium to do an interview for my nightly radio show, that we would tape in the afternoon. I sat down with Stengel, looked at my engineer and asked him how much time we had for this interview. The engineer said, "Thirty-five minutes." Casey heard that. When I asked him the first question, which was to analyze his team for that season, he proceeded to speak for thirty-five minutes straight. He'd heard the time, and helpfully gave me what he thought I needed.

One of Casey's many great quotes concerned the inept Mets of the early sixties, when he said, "Can't anybody here play this game?"

Which reminds me of something Danny Ozark, who used to manage the Philadelphia Phillies, once said: "Half this game is ninety percent mental." (Danny never was very good at the statistics side of the game.)

As a manager, Bobby Valentine, formerly of the Mets, is one of my personal favorites. He is married to Ralph Branca's daughter. Branca, you remember, threw the pitch that Thomson hit. Bobby is probably the best athlete ever born in the state of Connecticut, but his baseball career was curtailed by a terrible accident when he hit the wall going back on a fly ball in Anaheim. But he is an open, honest skipper. He knows the game inside and out, and he never gives up. Whenever the Mets came to play the Dodgers, Bobby joined us in the morning at Nate 'N Al's for breakfast, then we drove him out to the stadium and hung around with the team all day long.

What's the difference between a good manager and a great manager? Leo Durocher said it was about five games a year. Over the course of 162 games, that may not sound like much, but a lot of pennants are decided in five games a year. Earl Weaver told me that when you think about it, a manager is responsible for every game. He makes out the lineup and puts in the substitutions. Therefore when the team wins, he wins; when they lose, he loses.

I've had the privilege to interview many of the great managers over the years. Here are some quotes from the men who make those decisions every day.

EARL WEAVER

Earl Weaver, in retirement now in Florida, is a very good friend, and a man I spent many hours with at Oriole games. I loved sitting in the dugout with him during batting practice, listening to his wise words. He knew the game so intricately that I would absorb his vast knowledge just by sitting and watching the game with him and listening to his passing remarks.

The secret of being a good manager is to have thirteen men like you more than the twelve other men who don't like you at all. You must keep a majority, however slight, in your favor.

Jim Palmer and I had a father/son relationship. Whenever I took him out of the game he acted like I was taking away the keys to the car.

I always look at the schedule. I always want to know who we're playing next week and the week after; how many games apart are the teams in the division. You must think ahead in baseball. It is a thinker's game.

I think I've come up with a way to beat the designated-hitter rule. I haven't put it all together yet, but if I ever get the chance to try, it's gonna be a lollapalooza. I'm gonna find a way where I don't have a designated hitter. I might only have eight players in the game. I'll let the umpires figure it out.

It's not that I dislike umpires. They have a job to do, I understand that. I just can't stand when they do it poorly.

LEO DUROCHER

Willie Mays was the best ballplayer, the best athlete . . . just plain the best. I told him when he came up and I was managing the Giants to just go out and play center field. I never coached him, I never changed his batting stance, I never told him what to do or what not to do. I never saw him make a mental mistake. Not one time, not ever. Everybody makes physical errors—Mays made a few. But mentally? I never saw him throw to the wrong base, I never saw him not know who was at bat, or what the count was, or what the pitcher had thrown him the last time he batted. He may not have graduated from high school, but he was the smartest player I ever knew.

Sure I loved managing in Brooklyn. Then when I left to go manage the Giants, their hated rivals, that was pretty tough. But hey, I loved managing more than I loved Brooklyn, or more than I loved New York. So I had just as much fun there, and when Thomson hit that homer, I don't think I could have possibly been happier than that one second in my whole life. I was coaching at third and when I saw the bat hit the ball, I looked up into the left-field stands and thought I was going to die. It would have been OK to die then. I would have died with a smile.

I managed against other managers. I got to know their habits, tried to think what they would do in a particular situation, then tried to outthink them.

SPARKY ANDERSON

There's no secret to managing. Put the best ballplayers in the game and watch them play. Sit and watch them and have a good time. When you have to make a change, make the change based on all you've learned and all you know about the people you plan to change. It's not brain surgery; there's no trick to it. I thought managing in the American League in a world championship, as I did in the National League, was easier. The designated hitter rule leaves the manager very few decisions to make. With him the pitcher never has to bat, so the game plays itself more. I like the National League's rules better.

The most important thing to me was to be honest with my players. I'd never tell a player he was going to play tomorrow if he wasn't. Baloney doesn't work. Your players have to trust you. They don't have to like you, but they have to trust you. It's nice if they like you, but that's icing on the cake.

JOE TORRE

I understand that George Steinbrenner owns the Yankees and I work for him. He understands that I'm paid to manage his team. Sure he could call me up ten times a day. But George knows that wouldn't make any sense. If he doesn't like me, he can always let me go. I have no money invested in this team. But I love managing them. I've played a lot of baseball and managed a lot of baseball, and there's something about the way this team plays the game that always intrigues me. Sometimes I sit in the dugout and look out—I can't believe some of the things I see these athletes doing. Is there a Yankee mystique? I don't know, but I could make a good argument on both sides. I liked playing better than managing because as a player I felt more a part of what was happening. I've been playing baseball all my life. I think managing is more like directing a movie versus acting in a movie. I think an actor would rather act.

TONY LaRUSSA

I think being a lawyer doesn't hurt my skills as a manager. In fact, I would recommend that every person get a law degree. When you have a law degree, you not only have a better understanding of law, but you have a pretty good understanding of human behavior. What people do in a crisis, how particular situations are handled. In a sense, my players are my clients, and I'm there to guide them through the trial (a game). Every trial has someone against you—it might be another party in a civil matter or the state in a criminal matter. There are winners and losers in trials, as there are in baseball. That's why I think baseball mirrors life so well—it's a long season, the ups and downs are continuous, you win some, you lose some. One difference is, the jury doesn't decide the outcome. The flow of the game determines the outcome. The similarity is, in both cases there is an outcome.

BOBBY VALENTINE

I'm a very emotional person. I was as a player, I am as a manager. Japan was a great experience for me. Managing there required a lot of discipline. Watching another culture appreciate the game I loved, sometimes in a very different manner, gave me a broader picture. I never did get the hang of bowing to the umpire.

Mike Piazza is the easiest person I've ever had to manage. He brings his heart and soul and talent to every game. He gives it 100 percent. He never whines and I've never heard him complain. He's a true, true team leader. It's not generally known, but when we lost the last game of a playoff against the Braves once in Atlanta, Mike went to the car and drove across the country and back by himself, just to get the sadness out of him.

My toughest time was 9/11. We were in Pittsburgh. Naturally the games were cancelled and we had to come back by bus. As the bus approached the Holland Tunnel you could still see smoke in the sky. I was born and raised in Connecticut, but New York was my adopted home. As manager of the Mets I felt a great part of this city. I spent a number of days at Shea Stadium in the parking lot, which was set up as kind of a refuge station, handling supplies that had to go down to Ground Zero. I remember once we needed flashlights and Donald Trump had had a flashlight giveaway as a gimmick at one of his Atlantic City hotels. He sent all those flashlights to us to get down to the firemen at the World Trade Center.

You know who delivered them? Motorcycle gangs. A bunch of them pulled in; I thought they were going to kill us. Instead they said, "What can we do to help?" So we had them transporting flashlights all day and all night. It was something.

When we played our first game after 9/11 we lined up the Braves on one side of the field and us on the other. I couldn't stop the tears. I knew baseball was back, and it was important for people to know it. I looked around the stadium, looked at Mayor Rudy Giuliani's face, looked at the firemen carrying the colors, and listened to the National Anthem. I sat in the dugout and managed the game. We won on a Piazza home run. It was a night I'll never forget. It was important. We had come back. But it was still just a game.

YOGI BERRA

And, of course, who can forget Yogi Berra and his countless classic one-liners?

I always thought that record would stand until it was broken.

When you come to a fork in the road, take it.

No one goes there anymore, it's too crowded.

If the fans don't come out to the ballpark, you can't stop them.

You should always go to other people's funerals; otherwise they won't come to yours.

This is like déjà vu all over again.

Slump? I ain't in no slump. I'm just not hitting.

You can observe a lot just by watching.

I didn't really say everything I said.

And that, my friends, is the big question. Why is this game so important? Why does baseball affect me so? It has nothing to do with my income, my marriage, my fatherhood, my home, my culture, my life. Yet it is involved in all of them. I could go so far as to say it's an integral part of all of them. It's still just a game, 6 to 4, 3 to 2, 11 to 5, one to nothing. Ordinary scores in all sorts of places. You win some, you lose some.

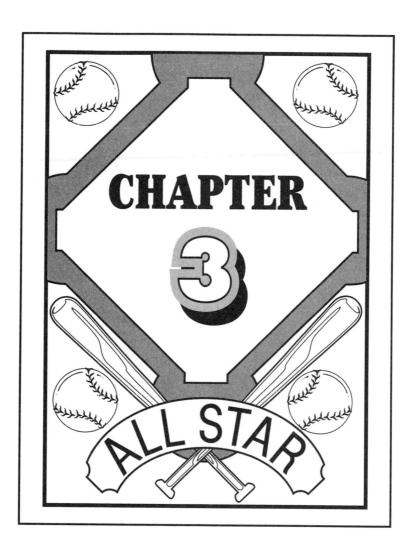

CHAPTER

3

ALL STAR

Baseball during the war years was a riot. The war years are considered 1943, 1944, and 1945. Somehow 1942 was a year in which a lot of the great players were still around, because December 7, 1941 had happened so late in the year, and our President, Franklin Delano Roosevelt, made the decision that baseball should continue. So a lot of the ballplayers didn't go into the service until the winter of 1942. In '42 the Cardinals beat the Yankees in five games, but the Musials and the Rizzutos were gone in '43 and did not come back till '46. The real boom year was 1947, when Jackie Robinson entered baseball. All the name stars were back, and baseball had resumed its place as the national pastime.

In 1946, there was a terrific World Series in which the Cardinals beat the Red Sox in seven games. That would turn out to be the only World Series that Ted Williams ever played in, and he did not have a good time. His batting average was a meager .200; indeed, so was Stan Musial's (.222) on the Cardinal side. The star of the series was Cardinal pitcher Harry Brecheen, who won three games, and Enos "Country" Slaughter, who played in the shadow of Musial all his career. He was one hell of a clutch player.

Anyway, during the war years most players were army rejects who were too old for the draft. There were even some players who were too young. Tommy Brown, the Dodgers' shortstop in 1944, was sixteen and a half years old. Then there was Joe Nuxhall, who pitched two-thirds of an inning for the Reds at age sixteen that same year. The games were pretty funny. Pete Gray was a one-armed outfielder for the St. Louis Browns. He had only a left arm, so he would carry the glove under his left arm. When he would catch the ball he would throw it up in the air, toss the glove off, grab the ball out of the air and throw it in. At bat he only hit .218, but that's pretty miraculous in and of itself. What do I mean 'only'? How did the man hit anything?

The Dodgers had a classic team. Elmer Valo was an outfielder who was deaf. Remember, these were army rejects, folks. Howie Schultz played first base. Howie would stretch for the ball thrown by infielders and sometimes have trouble coming back up from his crouch. He would lie prone on the field. Our second baseman was Eddie Basinski. Eddie couldn't hit and he couldn't field, but supposedly he was a very good violin player. Whenever he came to the plate all the fans would stand and pretend to play the violin. Our third baseman was Frenchy Bordagaray, who we think was fifty-six years old. Mr. Brown was our infantile short-stop. Our left fielder was Luis Olmo, a pretty good hit-ter. He once had a ground ball go through his legs, but continued the follow-through as if he actually had the ball in his hand. Brown "caught" it, then pivoted and threw to home plate, where the catcher kneeled down as if to catch the ball. Meanwhile the ball rolled on into left field.

Our center fielder was Goody Rosen. We loved Goody because he was Jewish. He was the star of our team. He wasn't good, but he was Jewish. Ah, but right field. Right field was patrolled by Dixie Walker, the peo-ple's "cherce" as they used to call him. Dixie had a brown bat and was a great hitter. For the life of me, I don't understand why he never went into military serv-ice. Dixie turned out to be a racist who tried to lead a revolt against the signing of Robinson and was quickly dealt off to the Pittsburgh Pirates at the end of 1947. We had a whole bunch of catchers, none of whose names stand out in my memory.

But if we had it bad, the Yankees had it even worse. The Yankees had players like Mike "Mollie" Milosevich, arguably the worst shortstop to ever play in the major leagues. They had a catcher named Mike Garbark. We used to laugh that Garbark broke DiMaggio's record in reverse. DiMaggio hit safely in fifty-six straight games;

Garbark failed to hit safely in fifty-six straight games. The Yankees had a third baseman named Oscar Grimes who was just hated by the fans. Maybe they hated his name, maybe they just didn't like the way he looked, but Oscar Grimes was so despised that once at Yankee Stadium, at the bottom of the eleventh inning, he hit a home run to break up a scoreless tie against the Washington Senators to give the Yankees a one to nothing victory. He was booed by the hometown team all the way around the bases. Now *that's* hatred. The Yankees had an outfield consisting of Herschel Martin, who we thought was Jewish because his first name was Herschel. Also, there was Johnny Lindell, a carryover from the '30s and Bud Metheny, who I have no memory of other than his name.

And the Giants were a raucous group of really old people. Walker Cooper was the catcher. Walker may have been 103 or 104. Johnny Mize was playing out his career, hitting the occasional home run. He joined the Yankees in 1949 and provided them with great help in their pennant drives over the next few years. Ace Adams was the Giants' relief pitcher. The great Giants star of the thirties, Mel Ott, played right field and managed. It was interesting when he changed pitchers—Ott would have to come running all the way in from right field to take the pitcher out, hand the ball to the new pitcher, then run all the way back out to right field.

Nevertheless, I loved the game during those years. I rooted for my seventh-place Dodgers in 1944. There were eight teams in each league then, so I always said Thank God for the Phillies, who usually managed to finish eighth. In those years the winner in each league played in the World Series. There were no wild cards back then, which I must admit does add drama late in the season. We were only kids, and we knew there was a war on, but we still loved our game. We used to sing war songs in the morning in class, like "When the Führer says we is the master race, we Heil phoo! Heil phoo! right in the Führer's face." We'd sing all the patriotic songs like "I Am An American" and "Over There." We'd carry our flags and give our dimes to the March of Dimes to help find a cure for polio, and, of course, "root root root" for the home team. We gathered around the street lamppost at night, looked up the box scores in the morning, and of course listened to every game we could get on the radio.

Baseball loves old-timers' games. Usually each major league team will present one on a Saturday or Sunday afternoon once a year, bringing back old-time players and setting up a kind of mock game. The Yankees have become most famous for this, bringing back Yankee greats to sometimes play Dodger greats or Giants old-timers or other rivals of the past. They usually play a three-inning game. These games have a lot of laughs, and it's great for the present-day fans to see their old favorites again. I remember as a teenager watching Joe DiMaggio after his career ended trotting out to center field to greet other stars who had played in the '20s and '30s.

The Crackerjack company used to sponsor an old-timers' game each year at RFK stadium in Washington where, much to my dismay, there is no major league baseball team. A good thirty to thirty-five thousand people would attend this sometimes raucous five or six-inning game featuring American League All-Stars of yesteryear against National League All-Stars of days gone by. I remember once sitting in the clubhouse with Joe DiMaggio, which was a great thrill, when in came some ESPN cameramen who were taking shots for their telecast of what went on in the clubhouse. DiMaggio was in an undershirt and was instantly incensed. He screamed, "Shut off those cameras! Don't you ever dare take a picture of me in an undershirt! If you're going to film me, you film me in my Yankees shirt. Nobody wants to see me in underwear." He couldn't believe they would actually do this. He looked at me incredulously and said, "Do you believe they want to shoot me in my undershirt?"

DiMaggio once said that one of the reasons he always gave 100% was that a fan sitting in the ballpark that day might never have seen him play before. He wanted to give him or her a thrill they would remember all their life. Joe was self-conscious about everything he did and every appearance he made. For example, when he could no longer swing a bat, he refused to wear a uniform at old-timers' games. He would arrive in a tailored business suit and wave from his box seat, but at no time would he step onto the field. For Joe to embarrass himself would be the worst sin of all.

There's a story about Ty Cobb at an old-timers' game being asked what he thought he'd hit if he were playing today. The greatest-average hitter in the history of the game said, "Probably .290 or .300." The reporters gasped. "Why so low? Is that because of night baseball, or increased travel, or greater pitching? Tougher demands on today's player?" "No," Cobb replied, "Because I'm seventy-one years old."

Once the famed Gashouse Gang came back to play an old-timers' game against the New York Giants at the Polo Grounds. The Gashouse Gang was a ragtag collection of former St. Louis ballplayers who won the World Series in 1934. They had more assembled characters on one team than any team ever. As the Gashouse Gang ran out to their positions, the first Giants hitter hit a ball to left field. Suddenly, the third baseman took a ball out of his pocket and threw it to first. It seems that every Gashouse Gang member had taken a ball with him out to the field, and they all threw them in at the same time.

Enos Slaughter once asked me before one of the Crackerjack games who was pitching for the American League. Slaughter would be the leadoff hitter for the National League. I told him Bob Feller. Both men had to be over seventy at the time. Slaughter fretted, "I'll bet he tries to crowd me." He was seriously worried about his at-bat appearance. It was on that occasion that Enos Slaughter told me a great story about Jackie Robinson.

Slaughter was born and raised in Arkansas and had never played with or against any black player. He had the kind of prejudice you would expect to come out of much of the South of that era. Slaughter told me how much he respected Robinson, and I asked why, since I knew Slaughter had had bitter feelings about blacks entering baseball. Enos told me:

> The first year Jackie came up he was playing first base. I hit a ground ball to second base and I beat out the hit and deliberately stepped on Robinson's ankle, drawing blood. I knew that he wouldn't say anything because his first two years playing he couldn't retaliate at all. So I got to second and kind of smugly stared him down. Two years later, I'm at Ebbets Field and Robinson's playing second base. I hit a ball off the right-field wall. I'm heading into second base which Robinson is covering. The ball is thrown into him and he takes the ball and slams me in the mouth with it, knocking out four teeth. I was spitting blood all over the

place. He looked into my eyes and said, "I never forget."
That son-of-a-bitch had my respect for the rest of my days.

One of the great joys of my life was knowing and interviewing Jackie Robinson. Indeed, I interviewed him about six weeks before he died. He was totally blind by that time. Jackie Robinson had all the courage and ability you could want in a human being and a player. I remember his first Dodger game in 1947. He had played the previous year in Montreal, the Dodgers' farm club, after signing a contract to be the first black professional in major league baseball. He was Rookie of the Year in the International League and Most Valuable Player in the Little World Series, where Montreal defeated Louisville. When he came on the field in his Dodger uniform, with that deep, rich black color against that white Ivory Snow uniform, it was a joy to behold. Jackie was amazing. He helped his team win the pennant, he was Rookie of the Year, we lost the World Series in seven exciting games to . . . guess who? The Yankees. Robinson went on to have a brilliant career, and when his true colors were shown, about two years after he started, we all got to see the real Jackie Robinson. He was a fierce competitor—one of his opponents claimed he would slide into his own mother to break up a double play. I asked him once if that were true, and he said, "Yes."

We kids never had any prejudice, we didn't understand why blacks weren't allowed in the game of baseball. We fully appreciated it as they started to come in. Larry Doby played in the American League, Roy Campanella came to the Dodgers. To their total discredit, the Yankees were very late in bringing along black players. The Boston Red Sox, too, were among the last teams to integrate. These have always been unforgivable acts in my mind.

Baseball's late entry into racial cohesiveness in the United States was a slap at all the leadership prior to Branch Rickey signing Jackie Robinson. There were blacks in professional baseball in the late nineteenth century, and there was never an official ban against them; they were just sort of weeded out and never came back in to the majors. Cap Anson, an outfielder for the Chicago White Sox, and a member of the Hall of Fame, absolutely refused to play with any "niggers," as he called them. In my opinion, he should not be in the Hall of Fame. That's just one man's view.

Baseball has changed quite a bit over the years. There are foreign teams in the Little League World Series. Cuba and Japan play the game superbly. The Dominican Republic supplies enough major leaguers to comprise two All-Star teams, and Latin America has become prominent in our national pastime. Today baseball is truly representative of America, and an accurate reflection of the melting pot that is our country. It sure wasn't in 1946 and before.

And baseball itself participates in the great melting pot. It links generations in a common love, a common purpose. It connects bygone days to our present day. Every sport deals with the past, but no other does it quite as importantly as baseball. You never see, or very rarely see, quarterback statistics measuring today's star against, say, Johnny Unitas. In baseball, they do it every day. At a game I am always remembering things I saw in my youth and comparing it to things I see now. The true fan knows all those little things and savors retelling the old stories to younger fans. For instance, did you know that the pitcher with the best lifetime record against the Yankees with a minimum of fifteen victories was none other than Babe Ruth, who of course twirled for the Red Sox before being traded to New York, in what goes down as the worst deal ever made, anywhere. It ranks right up there with naming a car Edsel, or even some business mergers I'd rather not get into.

CHAPTER

4

ALL STAR

As a Jew I always root for the Jewish baseball players. I think everyone instinctively does this. Blacks tend to root harder for the black players, the Irish Catholics usually root harder for the other Irish Catholics. Hank Greenberg of the Detroit Tigers was a ballplayer to die for. He almost broke Babe Ruth's record. We all swore that nobody wanted to pitch to him the last two weeks of that season because they didn't want a Jew to hold the home-run record. By the way, I still believe that was the truth, but hopefully times have changed.

When Greenberg hit his 58th home run of the 1939 season, he had two weeks in which to tie or maybe pass Babe Ruth, whose record stood at 60. All the stories at the time ran that because Greenberg was Jewish, the other teams, and indeed, the hierarchy of baseball, did not want a Jew to be the one to break Ruth's record. Greenberg was walked a lot those last two weeks. Teams were afraid to pitch to him. But Hank, to his eternal credit, always denied the rumors. He said that they pitched him carefully all season, and that he hadn't

walked any more in the last two weeks than he had previously. The records, I don't think, bear this out. Everyone believed the stories except Greenberg himself. In
his later years when he played for Pittsburgh he was
such a prodigious home-run hitter that left field at
Forbes Field was known as "Greenberg's Gardens."
When he hit a home run, the announcer would always
say, "Hank has just planted another one."

In my opinion, it's only logical to root for one of
your own. I remember wartime ballplayers like our
beloved Goody Rosen and Cal Abrams. Both of them
played for the Dodgers at the same time. Then there
was Sid Gordon, the Jewish third baseman for the hated
Giants. I always wanted my team to win, but I wanted
Gordon to get a lot of hits at the same time. We rooted
for Al Rosen, the great third baseman for the Cleveland
Indians. Of course we rooted for Sandy Koufax, who
today I am proud to call a friend. Nowadays, of course,
there are quite a few Jewish players in the majors, and
I find myself keeping an extra eye out for their comings
and goings and doings.

Shawn Green, the right fielder for the Dodgers, is a
current favorite of mine. He's a star player who does
not play on Yom Kippur. In fact, most Jewish players
decline to play on the High Holy Days, much to their
credit. I interviewed Sandy Koufax once, before a World
Series, and I told him we were going to broadcast the

interview on Rosh Hashanah, because I would be off that day. He said, "You must absolutely announce that this interview is on tape, because I won't play on Rosh Hashanah." We must have said it twelve times—this interview is on tape—because it aired on Rosh Hashanah.

In 1947, Jackie Robinson's first year, my friend Artie Sobel and I kept a day-by-day record of the Dodgers' season. We were thirteen years old, and we knew this would be a historic year. I would keep the book one week and Artie would keep it the next week. Each day we'd paste in the feature story from the *New York Daily News* written about that day's Dodger game. We would also put our own comments below the story. We never missed recording a game the entire season. The Dodgers went on to win the pennant and played as dramatic a seven-game World Series as has ever been played. The Yankees won it, naturally, but the two most-remembered plays of the fall classic were turned in by Dodgers.

The first was in game four, when the Yankees' Floyd Bill Bevens was pitching a no-hitter in the bottom of the ninth inning at Ebbets Field and Cookie Lavagetto broke it up with a two-run double in the bottom of the ninth to give the Dodgers a 3–2 victory. That's the game in which Red Barber said on the radio, "Friends, the Dodgers are beating Lavagetto to death at home plate. They are jumping up and down and hurting him so much with joy that Lavagetto needs a police escort to get away from his teammates."

The other was in game six of the series, with the Dodgers leading 8–5. In the seventh inning, Joe DiMaggio came to the plate against relief pitcher Joe Hatten. There were two men on base. DiMaggio hit a long drive into left center field that looked for sure like a home run that would tie the game. The Dodgers were in a must-win situation, trailing three games to two. Al Gionfriddo, who had gone into the game that very inning as a defensive replacement, started running with his back to the plate toward the wall. At the edge of the bullpen he made a leaping, one-handed, impossible catch that I still see in my mind's eye. Red Barber described it as "Gionfriddo goes back . . . back . . . back . . . back . . . back . . ." There must have been eight or nine "backs," as he followed every step. Barber exclaimed as Gionfriddo made the spectacular one-handed catch in that famous tone: *"Oh-h-h-h, Doctor!"*

We never put the final game of the World Series in the scrapbook, because the Yankees won. Our book ended with the sixth game, that 8–6 Dodger victory. I have no idea where that scrapbook is today.

Looking back, it amazes me that baseball was such a big part of our lives. We argued about it on the corner, dreamt about it. We'd buy every newspaper that New York had at that time: the *New York Times,* the *Herald-Tribune,* the *Sun,* the *World-Telegram,* the *Journal-American,* the *New York Post, PM,* the *Daily Worker*—yes, we got the Communist paper too, because it covered sports.

And we'd buy every weekly sports magazine that came out the minute it came out. We stood under the lampposts reading things to each other. We knew every batting average of every player at any given moment in the season. During the first two months of the season there were small-time bookmakers in high school who would pay you triple your bet if you could pick three players to get six hits. We'd put up fifty cents to win a dollar-fifty (my limit). I remember we always picked Frank Gustine of the Pittsburgh Pirates, who always seemed to get two hits every day in April and May. The contest wasn't any good after May, because by that time the wheat was separated from the chaff and it didn't make sense.

Along with following every move of the game, we'd also play our own versions of baseball. One was called punchball, with a rubber "spaldeen." Or stickball, with the end of a mop. Or squareball, which could be played in a confined area. All of these were street games; all these were part of baseball. I remember vividly when

Willie Mays, arguably the best player in the second half of the twentieth century, first came up as an eighteen-year-old. He would play a baseball game for the Giants in the afternoon, then go up to Harlem at night and play stickball with kids closer to his age. He was known as the "Say Hey Kid." He's past seventy now, and they still call him that.

As I said, the police took us to a lot of games, or we'd pay our fifty cents to sit in the bleachers. Every year the Yankees and Dodgers played each other in a three-game, preseason exhibition series right before opening day, which was usually on a Tuesday. The series would be played one game at Ebbets Field on a Friday, two games at Yankee Stadium Saturday and Sunday, and then they'd rotate the following year.

One Saturday preseason game was at Ebbets Field in Brooklyn, and it occurred on Passover. I think it was in 1948. I remember we brought matzo sandwiches, managed to finagle our way down behind the Dodgers' dugout, and gave matzo to the players. None of them knew what it was. Jackie Robinson ate a whole matzo square and then wrote down the name of the product so he could buy it. We gave Joe Hatten, the Dodger pitcher that afternoon, a big matzo sandwich consisting of chicken fat on matzo. This is not the world's healthiest diet, but it sure tasted damn good. Hatten loved it; he devoured it. He was also bombed in the first inning by the

Yankees, knocked out in disgrace. The ball flew everywhere off Yankee bats. To this day, I blame it on Herbie for giving Joe Hatten the chicken-fat matzo sandwich. Even though it was only an exhibition game it still hurt.

As any baseball fan knows, arguments are frequent and heated among lovers of the game. Each season Herbie and I would argue, position by position, who was better between the Yankees and the Dodgers. This would lead to vicious name-calling, yelling, and screaming. The only fistfight I ever had in my life as a kid was with Herbie. We were debating the merits of various Dodgers and Yankees that year—it had to be 1947. The catchers were close. First base was certainly an ideal position and each of us argued passionately for his team. We got to second base. Jackie Robinson, who was on his way to being Rookie of the Year, was playing second base for the Dodgers that year. A fellow named George "Snuffy" Stirnweiss, who won the American League batting championship in 1945 when he hit .309—that's how bad play was during the war years— was the second baseman for the Yankees, and a soon-to-be totally forgotten player.

When we got to comparing them, I said, "OK, that's one for me, naturally Robinson's better." Herbie said no, he liked Stirnweiss. I took his head and hit it against a lamppost. He punched me in the chin and down we went on the street. I was bleeding, he was bleeding; we never finished our discussion of every position and player. We didn't speak to each other for a week. To this minute I still can't believe he said that. I can still hear him saying "Stirnweiss is better." It was one of the all-time shocks of my life. It still rings within me.

Another time I entered a radio contest, sponsored by the New York Giants. I wrote a short composition. As one of the contest winners I got to go to a New York restaurant and meet Frankie Frisch, the Hall of Fame baseball player, who was one of the Giant announcers at that time. I remember they had frankfurters and hamburgers and all of us eleven- and twelve-year-old winners were thrilled beyond belief, even though we hated the Giants. Love and hate are intertwined in baseball, as they are in so many facets of life.

Though I was a rabid Dodger fan, my brother Marty, three-and-a-half years younger than I, didn't like the Dodgers for some reason. He became a St. Louis Cardinals fan. I have never figured this out. He became a Detroit Red Wings hockey fan; I have never figured that out either. Anyway, he became a fanatic Cardinals fan. Once we were sitting up in the center field bleachers, I guess I was sixteen and Marty was twelve-and-a-half. The Cardinals were playing the Dodgers. And what did we see? One of the Dodger coaches, dressed in civilian clothes, training a pair of binoculars at the plate and signaling to the dugout what the next pitch would be.

We were witnessing a baseball mystery—the Stolen Sign! My brother went nuts.

When we got home late that night, the Cardinals had lost. My brother knew what hotel they were staying in. He knew everything about the Cardinals. He phoned the Cardinals manager, Solly Hemus, woke him up, and told him of the nefarious activity of the cursed Dodgers.

Whether the Dodgers won or lost, one thing is for sure, the crowd in Brooklyn was always exceptional. Stan Musial, number 6 on the St. Louis Cardinals and the best hitter I ever saw, told me that Brooklyn was the best ballpark to play in, and that it had the best fans. Musial used to murder us, but at the same time we loved him, for his grace and for his ability. It was the fans of Brooklyn who nicknamed him "The Man." There was one game where Musial went five for five, and hit every outfield marker—he hit the left field sign, the left-center field sign, the center field sign, the right-center field sign, and the right field sign. His batting stance made him look like someone looking around the corner. There was no one like him. He *murdered* the Dodgers.

One other time, I remember going to a Dodger/ Braves Labor Day double-header all by myself. I don't know why I was all by myself, but I was. I guess I was sixteen or seventeen. The Dodgers won the first game, and I remember that if we had won the second game, we'd be tied for the pennant race. But Warren Spahn, that crafty left-handed Hall of Famer, shut us out. And the Braves went on to capture the flag that year.

Some years later I interviewed Warren Spahn, and he remembered every detail of that game. In fact, he remembered every pitch he ever threw in any game. By the way, Spahn gave up Willie Mays' first hit as a major leaguer, which was also his first home run. These are the things about the sport that absolutely floor me. The intertwining of the ages, the fact that it all eventually comes together and still goes on. Baseball is a game, as my friend Herbie says, "of models, myths, and memories." Its illegal activities and labor squabbles notwithstanding, its greed sometimes infuriating, nothing can take away from the joy of seeing a well-played baseball game. Even a poorly played baseball game ain't bad. As Bob Newhart once said about Pepsi-Cola, "I love Pepsi so much I'd rather have a warm Pepsi than a cold Coke."

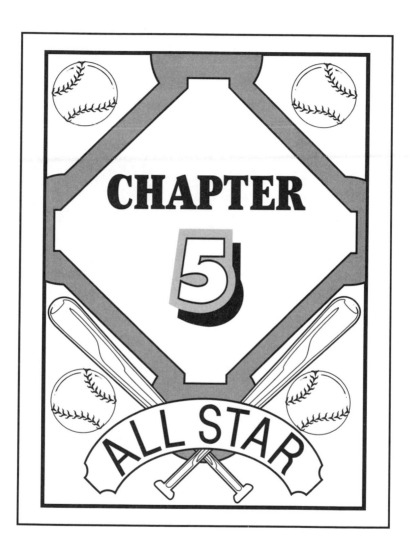

CHAPTER

5

ALL STAR

One of my great joys has been meeting my childhood herocs later in life. Getting to interview Jackie Robinson, Ted Williams, Robin Roberts—a whole host of stars from the past whom I watched in wonder as a child. Now I get to sit opposite a microphone from them and ask questions. Not a bad way to live.

Let me share with you some of my favorite quotes from players I've interviewed over the years:

JACKIE ROBINSON

Don't put me in my grave telling me that someday my people will have equal rights. Give it to me now, so that when I die I know they have it. I hate promises. . . .

Sure I had to suck it up those first two years. I knew there was a lot riding on me, and I knew the Dodgers had shown faith that I could control my temper until I had established myself and other Negroes were playing at the major league level. It was very hard, but I knew I had to do it. . . .

MICKEY MANTLE

If I knew I was going to live this long, I'd have taken better care of myself.

I guess you could say I thought I was the best, but in reality I think Mays was better. I think he could do little things better than I could. It's tough to admit, but I admit it.

TOMMY HENRICH
(the great Yankee right fielder known as Ol' Reliable)

I loved being a Yankee. I loved putting on the uniform every day. I loved touching the "NY" on my shirt. I loved standing out in right field at Yankee Stadium looking over at DiMaggio in center field, looking up at the crowd, realizing how lucky I was. Do I think that being a Yankee made me better? I'll never know, but it sure didn't make me worse.

JIM PALMER

I thought about every facet of the game when I pitched. Who was batting, who was on deck, what I threw them the last time. It's a very mental game between the pitcher and the batter. Every pitch has its own little story. Every pitch had a meaning. I would throw one pitch in anticipation of the next pitch. In my long career I never gave up a home run with the bases loaded. I gave up a lot of homers, because I was always around the plate, and batters knew they could dig in, but I never gave up a bases-loaded homer. I'd rather walk the guy. It was an obsession with me.

BROOKS ROBINSON

Baseball is a very, very difficult game. I loved the field, I wanted the ball hit to me. I had total confidence in myself when I was wearing my glove. At bat was a different story. I was a good hitter, not nearly a great hitter. I had some power, and I could hit in the clutch, but hell, I only succeeded twenty-eight percent of the time. That's not very good in anything but baseball.

PEE WEE REESE

I was a kid from Kentucky but I loved Brooklyn. I loved the fans, I loved the atmosphere at every game, I loved the band that came by to play every day, I loved the lady Hilda Chester with her cowbell, ringing it all over the stadium as she walked around. There were more characters in Ebbets Field than in all the other baseball parks put together. I'm sick to my stomach that we couldn't beat the Yankees more. But when that ball was hit to me in 1955, the ball that I would throw to first to end the World Series and bring, finally, a championship to Brooklyn—that game being played at Yankee Stadium was one of the great thrills of all time. I can still see Elston Howard swing the bat. Two outs, nobody on. I can still see the ball coming at me. I wanted it to come at me. I picked it up and there was

Gil Hodges standing at first. Howard was a slow runner; I had all the time in the world. I measured the throw, it hit Gil's glove, and life was beautiful, and there was a God.

Then there was George F. Will, member of the Board of Directors for the Baltimore Orioles and a lifetime baseball fanatic. I asked him once, how big a fan was he? And Will said, "If the *Washington Post* headline tomorrow morning said 'George Will's Secret Sex Life Revealed' I would first turn to the box scores."

To tell you the truth, I would do the same. I have done the same. Not about sex, but I've had stories written about me, some bad, some good in newspapers. I always turn to the sports section first before reading the story. If it's baseball season, I always check the box scores. As I write this, I could give you all the scores from last night's games. The winning and losing teams, even some of the winning and losing pitchers. It's hard to keep up with everybody with all the teams playing now, but that's how ingrained in me the sport is.

CAL RIPKEN, Jr.

Sure there was a lot of luck in breaking Lou Gehrig's consecutive game streak. I had to avoid injury, and that's lucky. I remember once I was sure I wasn't going to be able to play and the game got rained out. That was lucky. But maybe there was too much hullabaloo about playing all those games straight. Because when you think about it, I had a job for a lot of years for which I was very well paid. I was off in November, December, January, and February. I would report to Florida the beginning of March. My work time was an average of three hours every afternoon or evening, plus practice beforehand. That's less than the average American works. A bus driver has it much tougher than I do. He works eight hours a day, has to have quick reflexes as well, has people screaming at him at the same time. I would handle an average of maybe five ground balls a game and come to bat maybe four times. That wouldn't total five minutes of action. What's the big deal? It's a game. I love playing it. Sure I was the first one out on the field for practice. Why not? The sun is out, or the early evening lights are on, I'm a major league ballplayer making more money than I ever dreamed, the game is a delight to play . . . what's the big deal about that?

Speaking of Cal Ripken, Jr., I once asked Cal if he were starting a major league team brand new and he could have his pick of any one player in the majors, who would he choose? His selection surprised me. He picked Ivan Rodriguez, the catcher for the Texas Rangers who, he said, was the best catcher he had ever seen. He could not imagine any catcher ever being better. He picked a catcher because that is the mainstay of a ball club. He calls all the pitches. The field is in front of him so he's the only guy looking out at the field—the

other eight players are facing him. A lot of thinking goes
into being a catcher.

As I write this book, I am attempting to figure out why I
love baseball so much. What is it about this crazy game
that brings such emotion, such pleasure, such ups and
such downs, such joy, such despair . . . all from a bat
and a ball and a glove and a cap and a uniform? Such
memories. I remember when they had Ladies' Day, half-
price for all ladies. I remember double-headers. And I
vividly recall when night baseball first came in. I'll
never forget what it was like walking in, seeing those
bright lights hit the field. It was four hours of fireworks.
It was gorgeous. It still is. The first night game was
played in 1935 in Cincinnati and broadcast by Red Barber, who later would become the Dodger announcer.
But the first night game ever played at Ebbets Field was
in 1938 and resulted in a no-hitter. Johnny Vander Meer
of the Cincinnati Reds no-hit the Dodgers in the first
night game ever in King's County, New York.

Some time ago Barbra Streisand was considering doing a
CBS special called "Barbra Streisand's Brooklyn," in

which she would go around the borough and sing songs that reminded her of her youth, some original, some classic. Joe Raposo of *Sesame Street* fame was hired to write the tunes, and for a couple of days he and Barbra drove around Brooklyn as she recalled her childhood memories. They came to a spot at the corner of Bedford Avenue and Sullivan Place, where once stood Ebbets Field. It is now Ebbets Field Apartments, and the lobby of the building is the home plate that was once in the ground at that wonderful old ballpark. Anyway, Streisand looked up and said, "There used to be a ballpark right here."

Joe went home that night and wrote a song called "There Used To Be A Ballpark." The special never came off, so he filed the song away in his book of songs that were never released that all songwriters keep. One day much later Joe was at Frank Sinatra's house in Palm Springs. Sinatra was putting together an album called The Concert Sinatra. Joe had been hired on to produce the album and to write two original songs for the album. One of those songs turned out to be "Here's To The Winners," which I believe is played at the end of every Olympiad. But they couldn't come up with another song. Sinatra was leafing through Joe's book of unpublished songs and came across "There Used To Be A Ballpark." Joe told him the story, and Frank said, I love this song and proceeded to record it. Sinatra was the only person, to my knowledge, to ever record it. The album

sold well but the song is not famous. I recite it sometimes at the end of speeches, and it always leaves the
audience stilled. Sinatra told me that it was one of his
all-time favorite songs, because it says so much about
life, and why life is so much about baseball.

THERE USED TO BE A BALLPARK

And there used to be a ballpark
Where the field was warm and green
And the people played their crazy game
With a joy I'd never seen.
And the air was such a wonder
From the hot dogs and the beer
Yes, there used to be a ballpark, right here.

And there used to be rock candy,
And a great big Fourth of July
With fireworks exploding
All across the summer sky
And the people watched in wonder
How they'd laugh and how they'd cheer
And there used to be a ballpark, right here.

Now the children try to find it
And they can't believe their eyes
'Cause the old team doesn't play here
And the new team hardly tries

And the sky has got so cloudy
When it used to be so clear
And the summer went so quickly this year.

Yes, there used to be a ballpark, right here.

Now, in my humble opinion, you couldn't write any-thing like that for any other sport. You couldn't say, there used to be a puck flying through the air, or a bas-ketball once went through the net. Or there used to be a field goal right here. Only baseball. As George Carlin likes to say, "Baseball is special because you run to first, you run to second, and you run to third. But you don't run to fourth. You come home." *You come home.* You go into the dugout, the living room. The family greets you. You take a seat and watch the dancers.

There are many wonderful baseball songs. Here are three of my favorites from Terry Cashman.

COOPERSTOWN
(THE TOWN WHERE BASEBALL LIVES)
Words & Music by Terry Cashman
© 1982 PKM Music (ASCAP)
MetrostarRecords.com

How I hugged my daddy
When he gave me that old baseball glove
I think I slept with it that night

I loved it so much
I wonder if Hank Aaron started out that way
Dreaming of the big leagues and the Hall of Fame

I'm going to the place where baseball lives
Ruth and Cobb and Joe DiMaggio
Sunny days and Willie Mays
You'll be glad you took the trip
To Cooperstown, the town where baseball lives

A ball and a bat and some kids in an empty lot
We played till Mama called,
Hey hurry home it's getting dark
I read about "The Big Train" and Rogers Hornsby
They're part of America and they're part of me

I'm going to the place where baseball lives
Ruth and Cobb and Joe DiMaggio
Sunny days and Willie Mays
You'll be glad you took the trip
To Cooperstown, the town where baseball lives

Sunny days and Willie Mays
You'll be glad you took the trip
To Cooperstown, the town where baseball
Cooperstown, the town where baseball
Cooperstown, the town where baseball lives

RAIN DELAY

Words & Music by Terry Cashman
© 1982 PKM Music (ASCAP)
MetrostarRecords.com

There was sunshine on the diamond
Just an hour ago
What a day for a ballgame
Got me a hot dog and a Coke

Now they're covering up the infield
The umpire has called play
I search my pocket for my rain check
Lord I hate these rain delays

But life's a lot like baseball
If you know what I'm talkin' about
Sometimes you win, sometimes you lose
Sometimes you're rained out

Oh the sky's as black as midnight
Umbrellas spot the stands
But when the clouds are all cried out
I bet the sunshine comes again

Cause life's a lot like baseball
If you know what I'm talkin' about

Sometimes you win, sometimes you lose
Sometimes you're rained out

Sometimes you're rained out
Sometimes you're rained out

TALKIN' BASEBALL

Words & Music by Terry Cashman
© 1981 PKM Music (ASCAP)
MetrostarRecords.com

The whiz kids had won it,
Bobby Thomson had done it,
And Yogi read the comics all the while.
Rock 'n roll was being born,
Marijuana, we would scorn,
So down on the corner,
The national past-time went on trial.

REFRAIN:
We're talkin' baseball!
Kluzuski, Campanella.
Talkin' Baseball!
The Man and Bobby Feller.
The Scooter, the Barber, and the Newc,
They knew them all from Boston to Dubuque.
Especially Willie, Mickey, and the Duke.

Well, Casey was winning,
Hank Aaron was beginning,
One Robbie going out, one coming in.
Kiner and Midget Gaedel,
The Thumper and Mel Parnell,
And Ike was the only one winning down in Washington

REFRAIN:
Now my old friend, The Bachelor,
I wonder how he did.
Well, he swore he was the Oklahoma Kid.
And Cookie played hooky,
To go and see the Duke.
And me, I always loved Willie Mays,
Man, those were the days!

REFRAIN:
Well, now it's the 80's,
And Brett is the greatest,
And Bobby Bonds can play for everyone.
Rose is at the Vet,
And Rusty again is a Met,
And Alexander's pitchin' baseballs in Washington.

I'm talkin' baseball!
Like Reggie, Quisenberry.
Talkin' Baseball!

Carew and Gaylord Perry,
Seaver, Tommy John and Vida Blue,
If Cooperstown is calling, it's no fluke.
They'll be with Willie, Mickey, and the Duke.
Willie, Mickey, and the Duke. (Say hey, say hey, say hey)
It was Willie, Mickey, and the Duke. (Say hey, say hey, say hey)
I'm talkin' Willie, Mickey, and the Duke (Say hey, say hey, say hey)

Of course, there have been a lot of great books written about baseball. My favorite is *The Boys of Summer* by Roger Kahn, the story of the Dodgers in the late forties and early fifties. I read the book twice and interviewed Mr. Kahn on a number of occasions. I regard it as a classic work.

If you want to know about fathers and sons, read *The Boys of Summer* and watch *Field of Dreams,* and it will all come together for you. In that movie Kevin Costner caught the spirit of baseball through the eyes of a star. He needed to build that field and have all the old stars come back to regain his youth and square things with his dad. Baseball *is* fathers and sons. In fact, as I sit here writing this book at this moment with my son Chance on my lap, it is my fondest wish that he and his brother will grow up to be baseball fans—like their father, their uncle, and their grandfather before them. Of course, Chance might become a Dodger fan and break his father's heart, but even that would be all right, just as long as he loves the game. It is the one legacy I hope with all my heart to pass on to my boys—a love for the game.

George Will's *Men At Work* is another bestseller that deals with the lives of manager Tony LaRussa and ballplayers Tony Gwynn and Cal Ripken, Jr. It's a magnificent look at how the men of baseball do what they do; and of all the books Will has written, it was his biggest seller.

Jim Bouton's *Ball Four* is as good a read today as when it was first published in 1970. While it upset a lot of the baseball hierarchy because it revealed a lot of inside stuff, I took it as one very, very funny read. It still holds up wonderfully today.

The best book of baseball fiction I ever read was Bernard Malamud's *The Natural,* which was turned into a very successful movie starring Robert Redford and directed by Barry Levinson. The movie did cop out; in the book, the hero deliberately strikes out to lose the game and take the payoff. In the film he homers to win the game. Robert Redford cannot cop out. It was still a pretty good movie, but a much better book.

Still another great book I'll always remember is *Universal Baseball Association.* This was an incredible novel by Robert Coover. The novel is about an accountant with a boring job all day, but who had invented his own baseball game, which he played each night. He kept the stats of all the teams he invented and introduced players. He had been playing this imaginary game for twenty years. It affected his sex life and totally controlled him. It's been some time since I read the book, which I consider a classic, but I remember that as a result of a roll of the game's dice one night, his young phenom pitcher, who was well on his way to being Rookie of the Year in his imaginary league, was killed by a batted ball that hit him in the face. The accountant's life began to crumble. He had fallen in love with this imaginary player, but he would never change a roll of the dice . . . or would he? It was quite a read. If you can find a copy—it's still in print—do so.

As far as I'm concerned, reading and baseball go hand in hand. I read about it every day in the *Washington Post,* the *Los Angeles Times,* the *New York Times,* the *New York Post,* the *New York Daily News, USA Today,* and usually one or two other out-of-town newspapers. If the reader is getting the impression that I can't get enough baseball, you are very adroit.

Magazines are also very important to the baseball fanatic. I remember the premiere issue of *Sport* magazine back in the late forties. The picture on the cover was Joe DiMaggio posing with his young son Joe, Jr. both wearing Yankee uniforms. I would later interview Joe DiMaggio Jr. and found him to be one of the unhappiest people I had ever met. He passed away a couple of years ago. He told me that he had never really known his father, that Joe Sr. had been distant and remote. He had been flown in to take that picture for the cover of *Sport* from his private school and whisked away immediately after the picture was taken. He deliberately did NOT play baseball. When he enlisted in the Marines he called his father to tell him. His father said, "Fine," and nothing else. The only time they were ever close was at Marilyn Monroe's funeral. Joe Jr. loved Marilyn, and she was very good to him. Sitting next to his father in the hearse, they held hands. It was the only time they touched in their lives. I wish I had saved that front cover of *Sport*—it would be worth a lot of money today.

And in the early fifties along came *Sports Illustrated.* I can still see that first cover—Eddie Matthews, the Braves Hall-of-Famer swinging his bat at a game in St. Louis. *The Sporting News* was always our Bible. It was a weekly published out of St. Louis that covered every team, every minor league team, every aspect of the game. It was baseball fifty-two weeks a year. One of the proudest accomplishments of my life was writing a column for *The Sporting News,* which I did for six or seven years in the eighties. New management came in and swept us all out, but it was a lot of fun writing about the sport I loved every week. I now read *Baseball Weekly* every week, and I must admit it has replaced *The Sporting News* as my regular bill of fare.

Yearly editions are very important in baseball publications. These are the issues that come out around February. Street & Smith publishes one; Bill Mazeroski, the former player, has a magazine; there must be twenty of them. All of them deal with preseason prognostications—analyzing teams and players, making forecasts. I love poring through them. I must buy ten, maybe fifteen, at the beginning of every season.

Another staple at my home is Bill James, who usually turns out a book a year with his own unique take on the game. Bill has his own stats and his own way of analyzing each player. I interviewed James a couple of times on my old radio show and found him fascinating.

There have been many wonderful films about baseball too. I absolutely loved *Bang the Drum Slowly,* starring Michael Moriarity and a very young Robert DeNiro. DeNiro plays a catcher who is dying of cancer. Moriarity is the pitcher, the star of the team, and the movie takes you through one full season in both their lives. The late Vincent Gardenia is wonderful as the manager of the team. Moriarity plays a Tom Seaver type wonderfully well, and, of course, what do you say about Robert DeNiro. DeNiro would later make a baseball movie called *The Fan,* in which he played a wacko fan who attempts to kill baseball star Wesley Snipes. It wasn't a very good movie, but it was about baseball, so I watched it.

The Pride of the Yankees, the story of Lou Gehrig, starred a miscast Gary Cooper but nevertheless tugs at the heart. (If you ask me, Cooper was miscast because Gehrig was a very broad-shouldered hulk of a man, and Cooper was quite slim and wiry. He didn't look the part at all.) I've seen that movie a hundred times. And over twenty million people have claimed to have been there when Gehrig said, "I consider myself the luckiest man on the face of the earth." He said that two years before he died of the disease now named after him.

One thing I never get used to is seeing an obituary notice of a baseball player's death, someone I rooted for or knew. I knew Pete Reiser, Pee Wee Reese, Jackie Robinson, Gil Hodges, and Mickey Mantle. I knew Roy Campanella. It saddened me to read that "Spec" Shea, the old Yankee pitcher out of Connecticut who had one sensational year, died at age eighty-one. I can still see him pitching. Where have all the young men gone? Long time passing.

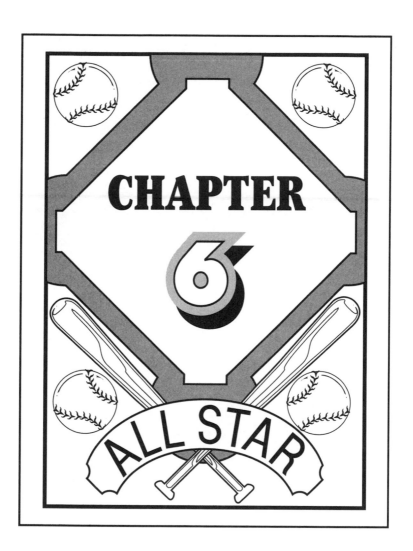

CHAPTER

6

ALL STAR

"WHAT MY FRIENDS SAY."

You've already heard about my friend **HERB COHEN**, who remains my best friend today, sixty years later. Here is what he remembered about the old days.

Remembering Baseball

When Larry King and I were kids in the Bensonhurst section of Brooklyn, we lived in a world of tar roofs, stone stoops, macadam paved streets and spaced manhole covers called "sewers." These heavy circular objects were used by us as a means of measurement.

It was how we determined the prowess of a slugger in punch ball or stick ball: "Hey, that spaldeen went two-and-a-half sewers. Wow, what a shot!"

By the time we were in grade school, we had discovered major league baseball, primarily through the colorful radio voice depictions of Mel Allen and Red Barber. Because of them, it didn't take long for the spontaneity, challenge, and joy of baseball to become an integral part of our lives.

From then on, spring did not come with the vernal equinox, but with the Yankee-Dodger exhibition game just prior to opening day. It was there in 1947, that we first saw Jackie Robinson in a Brooklyn uniform, playing first base.

Baseball was so interwoven in the fabric of our lives that it became our calendar. Summer kicked off with the Memorial Day doubleheader and autumn came with the start of the World Series.

Frequently, we would go to Ebbets Field, if we could scrounge fifty-five cents to sit in the bleachers. If not, we went free, courtesy of the Police Athletic League and sat in the upper deck in left field. Either way, coming from "the concrete world" of apartment buildings and small brick dwellings, it was always a thrill when we emerged from the darkened rotunda and saw the sun-filled playing field. For us, the immaculately manicured green grass, the rich brown earth—all symmetrically laid out, was our image of what heaven must be like.

On these occasions, we learned to appreciate that baseball was a game of strategy that required skill, endurance, judgment, and courage. In fact, we were there when Pete Reiser chased a ball hit over his head with such reckless abandon that he crashed headlong into the out-field wall. In those days, the fences were not padded and after a few of these collisions, the career of a great athlete ended prematurely.

One of the things that first attracted me to baseball was that it was a place where performance was what counted. While most of life seemed unfair, the national pastime appeared as the great equalizer. For on the diamond, wealth, status and even looks didn't matter.

Unlike golf, which was then an 'executive' game, or tennis, which was played in country clubs (there weren't too many of these in our neighborhood) baseball, we thought, offered models for community and excellence.

Of course, baseball gave us myths and memories along with heroes and history. But much more, it enriched our language with metaphors and even taught me mathematics. Specifically, how to figure a player's batting average in my head.

Above all, baseball teaches patience, perspective, and optimism. Although each ball game has a finite outcome, it's part of a very long season. In fact, the "pennant winner" will usually lose more than one third of the time. Even if your team didn't make it to the World Series, a real fan never lost hope. There was always, "Wait 'til next year."

Larry, a rabid Dodger follower in those days—even during the World War II years, when most of the talented players were in the military service, never wavered. Every November, he started regaling me with next season's future greats, such as Eddie "Banjo" Basinski, Gil English, and Howie "Stretch" Schultz.

And baseball helped us to become more tolerant and appreciative. After all, it's the only game where perfection is not expected and a sacrifice is applauded.

Throughout my life, baseball has been an inseparable companion, evoking the spirit of a more carefree past. But only from the time of Jackie Robinson and Larry Doby has it become the most American of all games—crossing barriers of race, creed, and generation.

CHARLIE BRAGG is a noted artist, a friend, and a lifetime fellow baseball fanatic. Below is his musing on the box score.

The Box Score

I'm sure that deciphering the mysteries of the Rosetta Stone, the Dead Sea Scrolls, and the ancient hieroglyphics was very important to the advancement of civilization as we know it. But none of them has had the lasting impact on my life as another marvel of eloquent and encoded information: the baseball box score. In 1942 at P.S. 82 in the Bronx I was introduced to that special code.

The deal was this: pick any three major league players and if they got a total of six hits between them a dime would win you fifty cents. The next day the box score in the newspaper showed the score, at bats, base hits, home runs, and everything necessary to recreate and understand what had happened to separate the winners from the losers. So thanks to the baseball box score I was introduced to the daily newspaper, illicit gambling, and advanced mathematics. Five cents x ten cents = fifty cents; that's five to one. Wow! I figured that out right away, just like a frigging 'A' student.

A sharp eleven-year-old handicapper like me would naturally pick out three great hitters like Stan Musial, Ted Williams, and the Yankee Clipper. It sounds easy. It wasn't. Try it. There's a reason Dickie Benz, our fourteen-year-old bookie, always had a pocketful of other guys' lunch money while most of the rest of us were walking around on empty.

Once in awhile you would win. My biggest score was an exotic trifecta of shortstops; Arky Vaughan, Luke Appling, and Johnny Pesky. I won big on that one, five bucks. Whenever he had to pay off though, Dickie Benz would also include a painful nuggie to the skull which took some of the enjoyment out of victory. He later became the CEO of a giant high-tech corporation. He'll be getting out of prison in about eight years.

In my day the players' batting averages would be published once a week in the Sunday papers. Now those averages are there every day. And that special language of the box score tells you what batters left men on base in scoring position, how many pitches a guy threw, strikeouts, walks, as well as who grounded into those rally-killing double plays. It's all there and crystal clear, for any baseball lover to recreate the game in his mind's eye.

As I get older it seems I linger over the box scores longer than I used to. I find it magical in its own unique way . . . and it also makes the news in the rest of the paper a little more endurable.

BOB COSTAS is a renowned sportscaster and friend.

I'll get to what I still love about baseball in a second, but to be truthful, my fondness for baseball has been tempered somewhat in recent years. The crassness and hype that infects most of sports has diminished baseball as well, although thankfully, there is relatively less of the mindless self-congratulation and belligerent posing that are so much a part of the NFL and NBA.

Still, baseball has other, larger problems that continue to damage or obscure its appeal. Debating the merits of players across generations has always been one of the game's unique pleasures. While each era brings changes in context, baseball always had enough continuity to permit reasonable comparisons among players whose careers were decades apart. Not anymore. Muscle-enhancing drugs and supplements, expansion, diluted pitching, livelier balls, harder bats, a shrunken strike zone, and hitter-friendly new ballparks have ripped the game from its historical moorings. Inflating the performances of everyone from the middling to the great. In the 30-plus years between Roger Maris's 61 home run season and 1995, there were three fifty-home run seasons. None higher than 52. Since 1995, there have been 18! (through 2002). That equals the number of fifty-home run seasons in the whole *history* of the game prior to 1995! In 1988, Will Clark led the National League with 109 RBI's. In 2000, 53 big leaguers drove in 100 or more. It's anyone's guess what the top players of even the recent past would do in today's distorted environment, but players who were in the big leagues for several years prior to the mid-nineties, and who were already established stars, have since put up numbers they never previously approached. It all feels somewhat distorted and inauthentic.

Meanwhile, baseball is saddled with a commissioner of dubious credibility and a players' association with little flexibility. Thus, much needed common sense reforms are never fully achieved, and an atmosphere of conflict and seeming contempt for fans pervades the sport.

Ah, but at least we still have the pennant races, right? Wrong. Pennant races were unique to baseball. They had a different competitive and dramatic character than mere playoff qualifying. The advent of the three-division, wild card format, has destroyed those unique characteristics. More teams may have a shot at it now, but this system precludes the high-end drama that once gave baseball's regular season its meaning. With the wild card as a safety net, it is now *impossible* to have a truly meaningful race for first place among any of the league's three best teams. Here's a fact, not an opinion: With the wild card to fall back on, no race for first, no matter how close it looks on paper, has any of the drama and meaning of the pennant or divisional races of the past. In 1996, the Padres and Dodgers, separated by a game, met on the season's last weekend. Same thing for the Cards and Astros in 2001. In a true pennant or divisional race, those games would have been brimming with excitement, riveting baseball fans everywhere. Under this system, the games were drained of drama. The wild card assured that next to nothing was at stake. A's-Angels in '02? The real race was for second – hold off third place Seattle, and you're in. Finishing first? Not that big a deal, as the wild card Angels went on to prove.

The notion that the wild card has added excitement to the game sends lovers of logic screaming into the night. You can like it, I guess, simply because you prefer more playoff games and more teams in the playoffs. But whatever excitement is generated by the wild card comes at the expense of the races for first. It's a trade-off, and not a very good one at that. Under this system, you don't even get the buzz of anticipating a great climax to a divisional race, because basically, it can't happen. This is progress?

So what's a guy to do? Here's what: Try to put these dispiriting realities aside, and focus on any or all of the following.

- A weekday afternoon at Fenway, Wrigley, Yankee Stadium, or Camden Yards.
- The combination of passion and civility that makes baseball in St. Louis seem so right.
- The strategy and maneuvers in the late innings of a close game (NL, without the DH, of course).
- Ichiro beating one out.
- Shawn Green (steroid-free) belting one out.
- Omar Vizquel diving into the hole.
- Tori Hunter leaping over the wall.
- El Duque's windup.
- Craig Counsell's stance.
- The classic form of Alex Rodriguez . . . and Don Zimmer.
- The sound of Vin Scully's voice.
- The memory of Jack Buck's humanity.
- The company of Buck O'Neill.
- The power of Randy Johnson.
- The precision of Greg Maddux.
- The presence of Pedro Martinez.
- A summer night in a minor league park.
- A bratwurst with secret stadium sauce in Milwaukee.
- Dusty Baker's sunglasses.
- Jon Miller's ties.

- A perfect drag bunt.
- A play at the plate.
- Teaching a kid how to keep score.
- The birds on the bat in St. Louis.
- The pinstripes in New York.
- The old English "D" on the hat of the Tigers.
- The Dodgers' home whites.
- Don Larsen and Francisco Cabrera—just one time, but it was the right time.
- The scene at Bob Uecker's boyhood home when a scout for the Milwaukee Braves declared, "We'd like to sign your son for $5,000," and Uecker's father replied, "This family doesn't have that kind of money."

I guess I still do love baseball.

Bob Costas
NBC and HBO Sports

Below is an article that captures so much of how I feel about the sport. It was originally published in the *Washington Post Magazine* in January 1987, just as the country was gearing up for the annual Super Bowl madness. Thomas Boswell laid out his reasons why baseball is so much better than football. I heartily agree.

WHY IS BASEBALL SO MUCH BETTER THAN FOOTBALL? LET ME COUNT THE WAYS.

Some people say football's the best game in America. Others say baseball.

Some people are really dumb.

Some people say all this is just a matter of taste. Others know better.

Some people can't wait for next Sunday's Super Bowl. Others wonder why.

Pro football is a great game. Compared with hockey. After all, you've gotta do something when the wind chill is zero and your curveball won't break. But let's not be silly. Compare the games? It's a one-sided laugher. Here are the first 99 reasons why baseball is better than football. (More after lunch.)

1 Bands.

2 Halftime with bands.

3 Cheerleaders at halftime with bands.

4 Up With People singing "The Impossible Dream" during a Blue Angels flyover at halftime with bands.

5 Baseball has fans in Wrigley Field singing "Take Me Out to the Ball Game" at the seventh-inning stretch.

6 Baseball has Blue Moon, Catfish, Spaceman and The Sugar Bear. Football has Lester the Molester, Too Mean and The Assassin.

7 All XXXVIII Super Bowls haven't produced as much drama as the last World Series.

8 All XXXVIII Super Bowls haven't produced as many classic games as either pennant playoff did this year.

9 Baseball has a bullpen coach blowing bubble gum with his cap turned around backward while leaning on a fungo bat; football has a defensive coordinator in a satin jacket with a headset and a clipboard.

10 The Redskins have 13 assistant coaches, five equipment managers, three trainers, two assistant GMs but, for 14 games, nobody who could kick an extra point.

11 Football players and coaches don't know how to bait a ref, much less jump up and down and scream in his face. Baseball players know how to argue with umps; baseball managers even kick dirt on them. Earl Weaver steals third base and won't give it back; Tom Landry folds his arms.

12 Vince Lombardi was never ashamed that he said, "Winning isn't everything. It's the only thing."

13 Football coaches talk about character, gut checks, intensity and reckless abandon. Tommy Lasorda said, "Managing is like holding a dove in your hand. Squeeze too hard and you kill it; not hard enough and it flies away."

14 Big league baseball players chew tobacco. Pro football linemen chew on each other.

15 Before a baseball game, there are two hours of batting practice. Before a football game, there's a two-hour traffic jam.

16 A crowd of 30,000 in a stadium built for 55,501 has a lot more fun than a crowd of 55,501 in the same stadium.

17 No one has ever actually reached the end of the restroom line at an NFL game.

18 Nine innings means 18 chances at the hot dog line. Two halves means B.Y.O. or go hungry.

19 Pro football players have breasts. Many NFLers are so freakishly overdeveloped, due to steroids, that they look like circus geeks. Baseball players seem like normal fit folks. Fans should be thankful they don't have to look at NFL teams in bathing suits.

20 Eighty degrees, a cold beer and a short-sleeve shirt are better than 30 degrees, a hip flask and six layers of clothes under a lap blanket. Take your pick: suntan or frostbite.

21 Having 162 games a year is 10.125 times as good as having 16.

22 If you miss your favorite NFL team's game, you have to wait a week. In baseball, you wait a day.

23 Everything George Carlin said in his famous monologue is right on. In football you blitz, bomb, spear, shiver, march and score. In baseball, you wait for a walk, take your stretch, toe the rubber, tap your spikes, play ball and run home.

24 Marianne Moore loved Christy Mathewson. No woman of quality has ever preferred football to baseball.

25 More good baseball books appear in a single year than have been written about football in the past 50 years. The best football writers, like Dan Jenkins, have the good sense to write about something else most of the time.

26 The best football announcer ever was Howard Cosell.

27 The worst baseball announcer ever was Howard Cosell.

28 All gridirons are identical; football coaches never have to meet to go over the ground rules. But the best baseball parks are unique.

29 Every outdoor park ever built primarily for baseball has been pretty. Every stadium built with pro football in mind has been ugly (except Arrowhead).

30 The coin flip at the beginning of football games is idiotic. Home teams should always kick off and pick a goal to defend. In baseball, the visitor bats first (courtesy), while the host bats last (for drama). The football visitor should get the first chance to score, while the home team should have the dramatic advantage of receiving the second-half kickoff.

31 Baseball is harder. In the last 25 years, only one player, Vince Coleman, has been cut from the NFL and then become a success in the majors. From Tom Brown in 1963 (Senators to Packers) to Jay Schroeder (Jays to Redskins), baseball flops have become NFL standouts.

32 Face masks. Right away we've got a clue something might be wrong. A guy can go 80 mph on a Harley without a helmet, much less a face mask.

33 Faces are better than helmets. Think of all the players in the NFL (excluding Redskins) whom you'd recognize on the street. Now eliminate the quarterbacks. Not many left, are there? Now think of all the baseball players whose faces you know, just from the last Series.

34 The NFL has—how can we say this?—a few borderline godfathers. Baseball has almost no mobsters or suspicious types among its owners. Pete Rozelle isn't as picky as Bowie Kuhn, who for 15 years considered "integrity of the game" to be one of his key functions and who gave the cold shoulder to the shady money guys.

35 Football has Tank and Mean Joe. Baseball has The Human Rain Delay and Charlie Hustle.

36 In football, it's team first, individual second—if at all. A Rich Milot and a Curtis Jordan can play 10 years—but when would we ever have time to study them alone for just one game? Could we mimic their gestures, their tics, their habits? A baseball player is an individual first, then part of a team second. You can study him at length and at leisure in the batter's box or on the mound. On defense, when the batted ball seeks him, so do our eyes.

37 Baseball statistics open a world to us. Football statistics are virtually useless or, worse, misleading. For instance, the NFL quarterback-ranking system is a joke. Nobody understands it or can justify it. The old average-gain-per-attempt rankings were just as good.

38 What kind of dim-bulb sport would rank pass receivers by number of catches instead of by number of yards? Only in football would a runner with 1,100 yards on 300 carries be rated ahead of a back with 1,000 yards on 200 carries. Does baseball give its silver bat to the player with the most hits or with the highest average?

39 If you use NFL team statistics as a betting tool, you go broke. Only wins and losses, points and points against and turnovers are worth a damn.

40 Baseball has one designated hitter. In football, everybody is a designated something. No one plays the whole game anymore. Football worships the specialists. Baseball worships the generalists.

41 The tense closing seconds of crucial baseball games are decided by distinctive relief pitchers like Bruce Sutter, Rollie Fingers or Goose Gossage. Vital NFL games are decided by helmeted gentlemen who come on for 10 seconds, kick sideways, spend the rest of the game keeping their precious foot warm on the sidelines and aren't aware of the subtleties of the game. Half of them, in Alex Karras' words, run off the field chirping, "I kick a touchdown."

42 Football gave us The Hammer. Baseball gave us The Fudge Hammer.

43 How can you respect a game that uses only the point after touchdown and completely ignores the option of a two-point conversion, which would make the end of football games much more exciting.

44 Wild cards. If baseball can stick with four divisional champs out of 26 teams, why does the NFL need to invite 10 of its 28 to the prom? Could it be that football isn't terribly interesting unless your team can still "win it all"?

45 The entire NFL playoff system is a fraud. Go on, explain with a straight face why the Chiefs (10-6) were in the playoffs but the Seahawks (10-6) were not. There is no real reason. Seattle was simply left out for convenience. When baseball tried the comparably bogus split-season fiasco with half-season champions in 1981, fans almost rioted.

46 Parity scheduling. How can the NFL defend the fairness of deliberately giving easier schedules to weaker teams and harder schedules to better teams? Just to generate artificially improved competition? When a weak team with a patsy schedule goes 10-6, while a strong defending division champ misses the playoffs at 9-7, nobody says boo. Baseball would have open revolt at such a nauseatingly cynical system.

47 Baseball has no penalty for pass interference. (This in itself is almost enough to declare baseball the better game.) In football, offsides is five yards, holding is 10 yards, a personal foul is 15 yards. But interference: maybe 50 yards.

48 Nobody on earth really knows what pass interference is. Part judgment, part acting, mostly accident.

49 Baseball has no penalties at all. A home run is a home run. You cheer. In football, on a score, you look for flags. If there's one, who's it on? When can we cheer? Football acts can all be repealed. Baseball acts stand forever.

50 Instant replays. Just when we thought there couldn't be anything worse than penalties, we get instant replays of penalties. Talk about a bad joke. Now any play, even one with no flags, can be called back. Even a flag itself can, after five minutes of boring delay, be nullified. NFL time has entered the Twilight Zone. Nothing is real; everything is hypothetical.

51 Football has Hacksaw. Baseball has Steady Eddie and The Candy Man.

52 The NFL's style of play has been stagnant for decades, predictable. Turn on any NFL game and that's just what it could be—any NFL game. Teams seem interchangeable. Even the wishbone is too radical. Baseball teams' styles are often determined by their personnel and even their parks.

53 Football fans tailgate before the big game. No baseball fan would have a picnic in a parking lot.

54 At a football game, you almost never leave saying, "I never saw a play like that before." At a baseball game, there's almost always some new wrinkle.

55 Beneath the NFL's infinite sameness lies infinite variety. But we aren't privy to it. So what if football is totally explicable and fascinating to Dan Marino as he tries to decide whether to audible to a quick trap? From the stands, we don't know one-thousandth of what's required to grasp a pro football game. If an NFL coach has to say, "I won't know until I see the films," then how out-in-the-cold does that leave the fan?

56 While football is the most closed of games, baseball is the most open. A fan with a score card, a modest knowledge of the teams and a knack for paying attention has all he needs to watch a game with sophistication.

57 NFL refs are weekend warriors, pulled from other jobs to moonlight; as a group, they're barely competent. That's really why the NFL turned to instant replays. Now, old fogies upstairs can't even get the make-over calls right. Baseball umps work 10 years in the minors and know what they are doing. Replays show how good they are. If Don Denkinger screws up in a split second of Series tension, it's instant lore.

58 Too many of the best NFL teams represent unpalatable values. The Bears are head-thumping braggarts. The Raiders have long been scofflaw pirates. The Cowboys glorify the heartless corporate approach to football.

59 Football has the Refrigerator. Baseball has Puff the Magic Dragon, The Wizard of Oz, Tom Terrific, Big Doggy, Kitty Kaat and Oil Can.

60 Football is impossible to watch. Admit it: The human head is at least two eyes shy for watching the forward pass. Do you watch the five eligible receivers? Or the quarterback and the pass rush? If you keep your eye on the ball, you never know who got open or how. If you watch the receivers . . . well, nobody watches the receivers. On TV, you don't even know how many receivers have gone out for a pass.

61 The NFL keeps changing the most basic rules. Most blocking now would have been illegal use of the hands in Jim Parker's time. How do we compare eras when the sport never stays the same? Pretty soon, intentional grounding will be legalized to protect quarterbacks.

62 In the NFL, you can't tell the players without an Intensive Care Unit report. Players get broken apart so fast we have no time to build up allegiances to stars. Three-quarters of the NFL's starting quarterbacks are in their first four years in the league. Is it because the new breed is better? Or because the old breed is already lame? A top baseball player lasts 15 to 20 years. We know him like an old friend.

63 The baseball Hall of Fame is in Cooperstown, N.Y., beside James Fenimore Cooper's "Lake Glimmerglass"; the football Hall of Fame is in Canton, Ohio, beside the freeway.

64 Baseball means Spring's Here. Football means Winter's Coming.

65 Best book for a lifetime on a desert island: *The Baseball Encyclopedia.*

66 Baseball's record on race relations is poor. But football's is much worse. Is it possible that the NFL still has NEVER had a black head coach? And why is a black quarterback still as rare as a bilingual woodpecker?*

67 Baseball has a drug problem comparable to society's. Pro football has a range of substance-abuse problems comparable only to itself. And, perhaps, The Hells Angels'.

68 Baseball enriches language and imagination at almost every point of contact. As John Lardner put it, "Babe Herman did not triple into a triple play, but he did double into a double play, which is the next best thing."

69 Who's on First?

70 Without baseball, there'd have been no Fenway Park. Without football, there'd have been no artificial turf.

* This was written some years ago. Now they have five.

71 A typical baseball game has nine runs, more than 250 pitches and about 80 completed plays—hits, walks, outs—in 2½ hours. A typical football game has about five touchdowns, a couple of field goals and fewer than 150 plays spread over three hours. Of those plays, perhaps 20 or 25 result in a gain or loss of more than 10 yards. Baseball has more scoring plays, more serious scoring threats and more meaningful action plays.

72 Baseball has no clock. Yes, you were waiting for that. The comeback, from three or more scores behind, is far more common in baseball than football.

73 The majority of players on a football field in any game are lost and unaccountable in the middle of pileups. Confusion hides a multitude of sins. Every baseball player's performance and contribution are measured and recorded in every game.

74 Some San Francisco linemen now wear dark plexiglass visors inside their face masks—even at night. "And in the third round, out of Empire U., the 49ers would like to pick Darth Vader."

75 Someday, just once, could we have a punt without a penalty?

76 End-zone spikes. Sack dances. Or, in Dexter Manley's case, "holding flag" dances.

77 Unbelievably stupid rules. For example, if the two-minute warning passes, any play that begins even a split second thereafter is nullified. Even, as happened in this season's Washington-San Francisco game, when it's the decisive play of the entire game. And even when, as also happened in that game, not one of the 22 players on the field is aware that the two-minute mark has passed. The 'Skins stopped the 49ers on fourth down to save that game. They exulted; the 49ers started off the field. Then the refs said, "Play the down over." Absolutely unbelievable.

78 In baseball, fans catch foul balls. In football, they raise a net so you can't even catch an extra point.

79 Nothing in baseball is as boring as the four hours of ABC's "Monday Night Football."

80 Blowhard coach Buddy Ryan, who gave himself a grade of A for his handling of the Eagles. "I didn't make any mistakes," he explained. His 5-10-1 team was 7-9 the year before he came.

81 Football players, somewhere back in their phylogenic development, learned how to talk like football coaches. ("Our goals this week were to contain Dickerson and control the line of scrimmage.") Baseball players say things like, "This pitcher's so bad that when he comes in, the grounds crew drags the warning track."

82 Football coaches walk across the field after the game and pretend to congratulate the opposing coach. Baseball managers head right for the beer.

83 The best ever in each sport—Babe Ruth and Jim Brown—each represents egocentric excess. But Ruth never threw a woman out a window.

84 Quarterbacks have to ask the crowd to quiet down. Pitchers never do.

85 Baseball nicknames go on forever—because we feel we know so many players intimately. Football monikers run out fast. We just don't know that many of them as people.

86 Baseball measures a gift for dailiness.

87 Football has two weeks of hype before the Super Bowl. Baseball takes about two days off before the World Series.

88 Football, because of its self-importance, minimizes a sense of humor. Baseball cultivates one. Knowing you'll lose at least 60 games every season makes self-deprecation a survival tool. As Casey Stengel said to his barber, "Don't cut my throat. I may want to do that myself later."

89 Football is played best full of adrenaline and anger. Moderation seldom finds a place. Almost every act of baseball is a blending of effort and control; too much of either is fatal.

90 Football's real problem is not that it glorifies violence, though it does, but that it offers no successful alternative to violence. In baseball, there is a choice of methods: the change-up or the knuckleball, the bunt or the hit-and-run.

91 Baseball is vastly better in person than on TV. Only when you're in the ballpark can the eye grasp and interconnect the game's great distances. Will the wind blow that long fly just over the fence? Will the relay throw nail the runner trying to score from second on a double in the alley? Who's warming up in the bullpen? Where is the defense shading this hitter? Did the base stealer get a good jump? The eye flicks back and forth and captures everything that is necessary. As for replays, most parks have them. Football is better on TV. At least, you don't need binoculars. And you've got your replays.

92 Turning the car radio dial on a summer night.

93 George Steinbrenner learned his baseball methods as a football coach.

94 You'll never see a woman in a fur coat at a baseball game.

95 You'll never see a man in a fur coat at a baseball game.

96 A six-month pennant race. Football has nothing like it.

97 In football, nobody says, "Let's play two!"

98 When a baseball player gets knocked out, he goes to the showers. When a football player gets knocked out, he goes to get X-rayed.

99 Most of all, baseball is better than football because spring training is less than a month away.

Thomas Boswell writes about many sports for the Washington Post. *He loves one of them.*

CHAPTER 7

ALL STAR

Baseball and radio are ham and eggs. Cats and dogs. They go together. Baseball's a perfect radio game. It's OK on television, naturally, because it's so wonderful to watch. But television can't capture its scope—it can't cover all nine positions at the same time. But baseball on the radio, as seen through the eyes of those men who made a profession of bringing the game into the mind's eye, is wonderful. When we love our hometown announcer, we love him. We don't like it if somebody else takes over for him for an inning or two. If you're a Dodger fan, you want to hear Vin Scully, just as the Dodger fans of my youth wanted Red Barber and no one else.

Believe it or not, we would even argue over announcers. The Yankee fans were married to Mel Allen. And the Giants fans had their beloved Russ Hodges. There was also Harry Caray in Chicago, Jack Buck in St. Louis, Bob Prince in Pittsburgh, Ernie Harwell in Detroit . . . people would sit on porches outside tenement buildings, on fire escapes with their portable radios, listening to the voices make the game come alive. As a kid I would listen to Red Barber and I swear I could see the game. His descriptions, down to minute details, in that wonderful southern twang, became as much a part of Brooklyn as Coney Island.

Late in his life I got to work with Red Barber at Channel 4 in Miami. I did interviews and he did sports. The first time he tossed it over to me, and I heard Red Barber say, "Larry, who's on tonight?" I thought I'd die. *Red Barber* had said my name. I interviewed him many times, as I did Mel Allen, Russ Hodges, and Harry Caray. Except for Vin Scully, they're all gone now. There are some very good ones around now. The extraordinary Jon Miller in San Francisco and on ESPN is my favorite. He has a great voice, an extraordinary sense of humor, and a wonderful manner of delivery. Bob Costas is right up there too, though he doesn't do the game much any-more, since NBC lost baseball lately. Joe Buck on Fox is terrific. And all of the Caray kids and grandkids carry on the family tradition—nobly, wherever they work—with a special nod to Skip Caray in Atlanta, who has lit-erally become a part of the Braves.

When I hear any of their voices I not only cannot turn the radio off, I become magically entwined with it. I am hypnotized by its rhythms, cadence, and pace. I've been in broadcasting for forty-five years and have, on occasion, sat in a baseball booth and broadcast an inning or two of a Mariners game or a Braves game.

Often I've had the opportunity to announce part of an Orioles game, and in each instance I always got a great charge out of it. I think if I ever left my CNN gig, it would be my dream to travel with a baseball team for a season and do the games on radio. I'd like to start in the spring, in Arizona or Florida, two nice places to be in the spring, and then spend a whole year with the ball club, at home and on the road. For me, that would be stealing money.

One night I was up in Baltimore's Memorial Stadium press box when Jon Miller was then doing the Orioles games, before moving on to San Francisco. I sat in with Jon in the broadcast booth. Jon was known for his dead-accurate imitations. He does Scully better than Scully. Jon said into the microphone, "I've been working on my Larry King imitation. I think I've got it down pat, so for the next half-inning I'm going to do it as if Larry were doing it." He then poked me on the shoulder and went to get a hot dog. I broadcast the half inning. I had to leave before the game was over to get back to the Mutual Radio network for my nightly radio show. At two in the morning I was taking phone calls from listeners. One caller from Baltimore asked if I had happened to hear the Orioles game that night, and I said no. The listener said, "Jon Miller did an imitation of you in the sixth inning." "How was he?" I asked. The caller said, "Fair."

One of the funniest people in baseball is Bob Uecker, voice of the Milwaukee Brewers for more than thirty years. Bob entered the Baseball Hall of Fame in 2003 when he won the Ford C. Frick award, given out annually to a broadcaster who has made major contributions to the sport. Uecker worked on network television when NBC had the baseball contract and, you'll remember, was the guy who did all those commercials where he always had a bad seat at the game. He also starred in the television series *Mr. Belvedere.* Bob was not a very good player, but he was always one of the funniest men around.

Here are just a few examples of some of his humor:

I signed a very modest $5,000 contract when I went into baseball. My old man didn't have that kind of money. But the Braves took it anyway. I remember sitting around our kitchen table counting the money, counting coins out of jars and telling my father, "Forget it, I don't want to play." "No," my father said, "You are going to play baseball." So I signed. The actual signing took place at a very popular restaurant in Milwaukee. We pulled into the parking lot right next to the team's official automobile and my dad screwed up right away. He didn't have the window rolled up far enough, and our tray fell off and all our food landed on the ground. That's the kind of restaurant it was.

Everybody remembers their first game in the Major League. I can remember walking out on the field. Birdie Tebbetts was our manager. My whole family was there. Everybody was standing on the field, waving at me and laughing. I was pointing and waving back. Tebbetts came up and asked me if I was nervous or uptight. I said, "No, I'm ready to go. I've been waiting five years to get here." He said, "Well, you're going to play today. I didn't want to tell you earlier because I didn't want to get you too fired up." "I'm ready to go!" I told him. "Great," Tebbetts said. "Oh, by the way, the rest of us up here wear our jock supporter on the inside."

I'll never forget the day I was released from baseball. It was very tough on me. Luman Harris was the manager. He came up to me in the clubhouse and said, "No visitors allowed."

In my life, on occasional visits to Vegas, I have bet on a total of maybe ten baseball games. Despite my self-believing knowledge, I probably won five and lost five. Baseball is a very hard game to bet on. So much depends on the pitcher that day, and it is all a guessing game. It is less heavily bet on now than it used to be, but it still brings quite a bit of action to the sports books.

My friend Bob Costas tells a classic story of the baseball bettor. His father was a total gambler. He would bet on whether a man or a woman would come off a bus first. One day Costas and his father are watching television. His father has bet a parlay; that is, he has bet on two teams, and both must win their games for him to win his bet. He has bet the Yankees, who are playing the Red Sox, and he has bet the Tigers, who are playing the Indians. The Tigers and Indians are involved in a double header.

His father stipulates that Lolich, Mickey Lolich, must pitch the first game. He's betting the Tigers and the Yankees—they both must win, but Lolich must pitch. If Lolich does not pitch in the first game, then he bets on Lolich on the second game. That's the condition of the parlay. Okay, back to the story. Costas and his father are watching. The Yankees have taken an immediate lead over the Red Sox and are coasting to victory. As the camera pans the scoreboard, the father notices that at the top of the first inning in the first game at Detroit, the Indians have scored eight runs. He is now praying that Lolich is going to pitch the second game.

Phil Rizzuto, broadcasting the Yankee game, suddenly says, "Holy cow! In Detroit today in the first game of a double header, Cleveland has scored eight runs and knocked out Mickey Lolich." His father becomes the most depressed person in the world. He sits there morose as the game continues. He notices on the scoreboard that Detroit is pecking away—they score one run in the third inning, two runs in the fifth, three in the sixth. When they get to the bottom of the ninth, Detroit now trails 8–6. Suddenly, Rizzuto says, "How about that! After giving up eight runs in the first inning, knocking out Lolich, Detroit holds Cleveland scoreless the rest of the way, gets three runs in the bottom of the ninth and wins 9–8." Costas's father jumps up and says, "Did I tell you Lolich, or what?"

That's a classic gambling story, and a great baseball story too. And all too true if you know your way around betting.

I haven't talked about umpires much, but they are certainly a necessary part of the game. Once, for a brief time in my life, I thought I would like to become an umpire, but I always wore glasses and I figured that it would be impossible. I would umpire some softball games with the older guys who were in a league in my neighborhood and always enjoyed it. You feel in such complete command. You are the arbiter, the final word, the judge, the jury, the Supreme Court. When you said safe it meant SAFE. When you said strike one it was STRIKE ONE.

The umpires goofed a few years ago, when they listened to union leadership and resigned en masse, thinking it would prod management to meet their demands. Instead they all got fired, the courts upheld it, and only about half have returned. It was a sad day in labor history. Like I said, I've always supported labor, and I've always supported umpires in their fights for better wages and conditions. They have a thankless job, and I've gotten mad at them when replays showed them wrong. But it doesn't happen that often.

For a long time umpires were either National League umpires or American League umpires. American League umpires at home plate would wear a chest protector in front of them; National League umpires would wear theirs under their jacket and not inflate it as much. Now there are no separate leagues with different presidents, and all umpires are under one contract and work both leagues throughout a season.

They're talking about new machinery now that will be able to correct an umpire's mistakes on balls and strikes. Umpires vehemently protest this. I feel a little mixed about the whole idea. If the technology is 100%, then I'd use it. What's wrong with getting everything right?

When we were kids and the umpires came onto the field at Ebbets Field the organ would play *Three Blind Mice*. At that time only three umpires worked a game; now there are four. We loved, and still love, watching managers argue with umpires. Arguments are great in baseball. They don't happen in football, because there you're not allowed to argue. In hockey if you yell from the bench you get penalties. In basketball you get technical fouls. But in baseball they jaw at each other for minutes on end before somebody gets tossed. I love a good argument.

Baseball fights are funny, because nobody ever really fights. When the batter thinks the pitcher throws at him he charges the mound and they fall into each other's arms before anybody can get hit. Most of the other players come running to stand and watch the incident, which is maybe a light push, a gentle shove. In hockey it would be a mad brawl.

In fact, I think baseball is the most civilized of team sports. I'm so used to yelling that once Herbie Cohen and I were at a tennis match at La Costa watching the pros on the Women's Tour. We started yelling "Come on, hit the ball!" The umpire (they're called umpires in tennis too) threw us out of the stadium. We were sixty-six years old at the time. Such behavior comes from growing up with baseball.

I've always been fascinated by baseball uniforms. They are so much a part of me that when I click on the television—and yes, I do have a satellite dish so I can get as many games as possible—I can immediately recognize who's playing, just by seeing the uniforms. By the way, on the night before President Bush's inauguration, I emceed a big get-together at the Lincoln Memorial. Walking off with the then-president-elect, he turned to me and said, "Do you believe there's no satellite dish at the White House? How am I going to watch Ranger games?" Apparently the White House did not have DirecTV. I'm sure this oversight was quickly corrected. The President is as wacko about the sport as I am.

More recently, I was at the White House for an hour interview with Laura Bush just prior to Christmas 2003. The First Lady gave me a tour of the White House and an in-depth interview as well. At the end of the interview, as we were standing in front of the gingerbread house, out walked the President. It was meant to surprise me, and it did. I asked him if he was full of surprises this year. He said he sure was. Baghdad, *Larry King Live,* you name it. I asked him about Iraq and a few other items in the news, and we closed the show with the President, First Lady and I wishing everybody a happy holiday. The second the program ended and the red light went off on the camera, the President turned to me and said, "What do you hear from the Red Sox? Do you think they'll get A-Rod?" Once a baseball fan, always a baseball fan.

But back to the uniforms. I think I've already said that the Dodgers had the crispest white uniform I've ever seen, the whitest white. They still have the whitest white, and they still have "Dodgers" written in script across the front of their chest. It has been that way ever since I've known the team. The only thing that changed on the cap was the "B" to "LA." Their road uniform has always been the same color, gray.

The Yankees uniforms have never changed—their names have never gone on the back. White with pinstripes, kind of boring gray road uniforms that say "New York" on the front. Baseball uniforms used to be flannel. Can you imagine that? Flannel in the summer. We never thought of what that must have been like. Today's modern fabrics make all the uniforms feel cool.

The Giants had a totally nondescript uniform while in New York, but in San Francisco they probably have the best uniforms now in all of sports. In fact, the Men's Designer's Guild of America voted the San Francisco Giants as having the best uniform in sports. It has a wonderful combination of white and brown and orange at home; gray, brown, and orange on the road. The "S" overlaps the "F"—it's beautiful.

The Oakland A's were the first team to radically change uniforms, under their late owner Charlie Finley. The A's wore green and yellow. They looked weird. The Houston Astros then followed suit with the strangest color combination I'd ever seen—bright orange and white, with sort-of stripes across the center. The team started wearing white sneakers when they played on artificial turf. The White Sox played a season with short pants at home when the weather was hot. It was strange. Maybe I'm a conventional person at heart when it comes to baseball, but I like my home white and my road gray, though I must admit I do like it when the Mets wear black. So, too, the Orioles, my two favorite teams. Black was unheard-of in the 60s and 70s as a color for a team. For the Chicago Bears football team, yes, but for a baseball team, no. Now it looks nice.

Cub uniforms haven't changed. The Atlanta Braves have gone from a kind of weird circular blue and white to a very nice takeoff on the old Boston Brave uniforms of the 1940s. The Boston Braves were the predecessor to the Atlanta Braves, with a stop in Milwaukee in between. I always liked the way the Tigers print their "D." The California Angels uniform seems to change every year. And I love, absolutely love the Cardinals' uniform. The two birds sitting on a baseball bat have been there since the 1920s, and never lose their attractiveness to me. The Cardinal red hats always seem to be just right. Anyway, as you can see I'm a uniform freak.

I'm also a ballpark freak. Baseball stadiums are much more famous than football stadiums. Let's face it, there are no famous football stadiums. They all look the same, don't they? Indoor arenas, except for maybe the storied Madison Square Garden, are only known for their histories, rather than for anything special about the buildings themselves.

But baseball parks are part of legend. The old parks are no more: Ebbets Field, Crosley Field, Briggs Stadium, the Polo Grounds, Forbes Field, Shibe Park, Memorial Stadium in Baltimore, Sportsman's Park in St. Louis . . . all are gone now, but all live distinctly in my mind.

Now even the newer baseball stadiums try to capture the uniqueness of the old ones. Camden Yards in Baltimore started the trend. It looks like a combination of Wrigley Field in Chicago and three or four other old-time ballparks. I was there on opening day and I will never forget it. I remember one of the players telling me that he feels like he's living in the past when he runs out onto the turf at Camden Yards.

That's another great thing about the sport—there are no official rules concerning the field. Other than the distance between the bases, my stadium can have thirty thousand seats, yours can have sixty. My distance to right field can be 320 feet and yours can be 420 feet. You can have a dome on top and I don't have to. Every little ballpark has its own nuance, crazy little ground rules that affect that stadium only. Football fields, basketball courts, and hockey rinks are all identical, with some few hockey exceptions. But there is no park like Fenway Park in Boston, with its giant left-field wall, or Wrigley in Chicago with the vines growing in the outfield, or Chavez Ravine in Los Angeles—funny, that's now considered an older park—with the palm trees and mountains in the background.

The newer stadiums, after Baltimore, include Pittsburgh, Texas, San Francisco, Milwaukee, Detroit, and Cleveland, as well as the SkyDome in Toronto and the remodeled Edison Field for the Anaheim Angels. Everyone has their own favorite. The consensus is that Pac Bell by the San Francisco Bay is the prettiest. Needless to say, each one has its own grace, its own stature, its own specialness. I get the same feeling when I walk into any one of them. Thomas Wolfe said you can't go home again. You can. Go to a game.

CHAPTER

8

ALL STAR

Baseball is a game you can discuss all year long. The Hot Stove League, as we call it, is where you discuss trade rumors and stories of the past season and hopes for the upcoming season during the long winter months. It produces great arguments and conjecture. There are winter meetings for general managers and owners and unions. All this is covered extensively in the press and devoured by us fans, who do not stop loving the game because it isn't being played November through February. We know all the intangibles.

Come to think of it, it's really only off for four months. Because spring training games start around the first of March, and the World Series ends in late October.

Of all the major sports in America, it's the only one whose preseason perks me up. I follow the doings every day of the young rookies. How are the old guys holding on? I remember as a kid in Brooklyn when it would be snowing outdoors and Red Barber would be describing Vero Beach and the sun, 78 or 82 degrees. I would fantasize what that must be like. Wow, baseball in March!

When I wound up living in Miami I attended as many spring training games as I could, because I love the sound of the bat and the ball. I love seeing all the youngsters, and the old guys trying to hang on for one more season. The new guys coming along, I liked to predict who'd make it and who wouldn't. The best thing about spring training is that hope springs eternal in all teams. Everybody is 0 and 0. It doesn't matter if you win or lose an exhibition game, only how well did the third baseman look? How did that new pitcher twirl?

This past winter was a classic example of how baseball is sometimes as interesting in the off-season as it is during the regular season. Here we had the possible trade of the best player in the game, A-Rod, Alex Rodriguez, from the Texas Rangers to the Boston Red Sox—so Nomar Garciaparra could go from Boston on to the Chicago White Sox or maybe the Los Angeles Dodgers. And where would Manny Ramirez wind up? With so many possibilities, speculation was endless and constant. There was grist for the mill every day in the sports pages and beyond, leading to many discussions at water coolers across the country.

And then, of course, came the Pete Rose eruption in January, when Pete came out of the closet, so to speak, to admit after fourteen years of lying that yes, he had bet on baseball games and his own team while managing the Cincinnati Reds. He continued to deny betting from the clubhouse or ever betting against his own team.

I can only imagine what it must have been like when Rose got together with the publishers of his book and they planned its release. His appearance on *Good Morning America* came out looking planned and contrived, and his regrets didn't seem all that regretful. And the timing seemed to deliberately take attention away from the news about the year's Hall of Fame inductees. This caused Rose to apologize to both Paul Molitor and Dennis Eckersley, who went into the Hall of Fame but had their moments of glory overshadowed by the fact that all anyone could talk about was Rose.

Pete Rose is a really tragic case in the sense that given his achievements, the man was certainly deserving of being in the Hall of Fame. On his record alone, he should be in—but if he's in, then "Shoeless" Joe Jackson should be in also. "Shoeless" was found not guilty of throwing the 1919 World Series—a Series in which he hit over .400. "Shoeless" Joe, who could not read or write, belongs in the Hall of Fame; he was a victim of circumstance. Rose created his own set of circumstances. It is my opinion that both should both be in the Hall of Fame, but I don't think that Rose should be allowed back in baseball again, certainly not to manage. We could never put our full trust in him again, given that kind of decision-making.

So, on balance, put him in the Hall of Fame, and let the plaque read what he did: that he bet on baseball. Whatever happens, once again it proves my theory that baseball is as interesting in January as it is in August.

Baseball owners were always well known over the years by the team's fans. Some were really well-liked. Tom Yawkey in Boston always paid his players well, and while the Red Sox didn't always win, the fans knew that Yawkey really cared and tried hard to produce a winning team. William Wrigley in Chicago had his beloved Cubs. His gum company gave him deep pockets, and he tried like hell to make his team a winner. Unfortunately, he could not.

In Brooklyn, we knew Walter O'Malley, and when he pulled the team out of the city and moved them to Los Angeles, he became the most hated man ever in the history of the borough. That hatred remains today. Whenever I see his son Peter (Walter died some years ago) I greet him warmly, because I like him a lot, but I always think of his father.

Horace Stoneham moved the Giants out of New York at the same time O'Malley moved the Dodgers out of Brooklyn. Giants fans hated him too. He was known as a heavy drinker who didn't pay much attention to what was going on around him. It was generally felt that O'Malley had lured him to go west.

Charlie Finley was a character in both Kansas City and Oakland, but he did win three pennants and three World Series in a row with the A's. Even though he won with the team and had some great ballplayers, I don't think the fans ever really warmed up to him.

George Steinbrenner in New York is not adored by the press, but I think the Yankee fans love him. He spends his money, brings them winners, and that's what the fans want—winners. When my late dear friend Edward Bennett Williams first bought the Orioles, Baltimore fans were not trusting of him. They thought he planned to move the team to Washington. Ed not only kept the team in Baltimore but brought them a world championship in 1983. They held a parade in which he was roundly cheered.

Bill Veeck was a popular owner because of his gimmicks. His attempts to please the crowd were always appreciated. One of the funniest moments in baseball history was when Veeck's St. Louis Browns signed a midget, Eddie Gaedel. They got his name on the roster for a Sunday double-header with the Detroit Tigers and announced him as the leadoff hitter when the second game began. The crowd went nuts. The umpire went crazy.

The pitcher, Bob Cain, got down on his knees to throw the pitch. The catcher sprawled prone to catch the pitch. Gaedel walked on four straight high pitches. It would have been impossible to throw a strike. Gaedel was mad that they didn't give him a pitch to hit. A runner was sent in for him, and Gaedel's career was complete. This stunt was Bill Veeck's idea. He was always thinking of different gimmicks to enhance the game of baseball. He would have cow-pulling contests before the game to draw milk. He once had his fastest player run a race against a horse before a game to see who would win. The player took the lead, but the horse won out in the late stages. Veeck would do anything.

Nowadays a lot of corporations own teams. Fox owns the Dodgers—who is Fox? The Chicago Tribune Company owns the Cubs. Quick—name the president of the Cubs.

Baseball writers sometimes really get on my nerves. I wonder whether they like the sport as much as I do. The manner in which they treat some players is beyond understanding. Let me explain. I firmly believe that how a player treats a writer makes no difference in the world at all about anything. All a player owes a fan is his best performance on the field. He doesn't owe the writer an interview; he doesn't even have to be nice to the writer.

He doesn't even have to know the writer exists. All he has to do is play ball.

But the writers take it personally. I remember once having dinner with Mike Lupica, the excellent *New York Daily News* sportswriter and sometime novelist. We were discussing St. Louis Cardinal pitcher John Tudor. Apparently Tudor was a very, very difficult guy to get along with from the writers' standpoint, and Lupica was trying to get me to not like Tudor because of the way Tudor treated him. I told him I didn't know Tudor, and I like Mike, so I was willing to accept everything he said about Tudor. But as a fan, Tudor was one hell of a pitcher, and that's all that should have counted to St. Louis Cardinals fans at the time.

Who really cares if Tudor likes Lupica or Lupica likes Tudor? All I care about is how well does Lupica write and how well does Tudor play?

Barry Bonds is another excellent case in point. I have never had one bad moment with Bonds. He's been on my show, I've been out with him socially, I find him ingratiating, warm, open, honest; yet a lot of writers and broadcasters find him to be a turnoff, a braggart, above it all, a lonesome dove, and so on. So what? If the writer or the broadcaster doesn't like Bonds, fine, what do I care? All I care about is how well does Bonds play? Does he give his all when he plays?

This has been historically true not only in baseball but in all sports. If the writer or the broadcaster doesn't like the athlete, he will try to cook him in the mind of the public. There's a lot of hypocrisy involved here. Writers claim they want honesty. But when they get athletes who are often directly and harshly honest, they get mad at the athlete. They like the goody-two-shoes type, who plays up to them to get good press. None of this—I repeat, NONE OF THIS—has anything to do with performance. To me, the fan, performance is all that counts. Sure I care if a player is arrested or in some kind of trouble with the law, and naturally that is some kind of a story, since the player is a public person. But how the player treats a writer who is covering him is irrelevant.

It's different in politics. A politician is paid by the public and owes it to discuss things with the people who cover him or her. That's not true in baseball or any sport. Frank Sinatra once told me, "What I owe an audience is my absolute best performance every time I go on the stage, into a recording studio, or before a camera. I owe that to me and to my audience. Anything else is gravy." Amen.

The labor situation in baseball is very sad to me, a lover of the game. I want to see it played; I never want to see it stopped. When baseball has stopped in the past, it's like shutting off an artery to me. Basically it comes down to millionaires arguing with billionaires. I'm a union guy. I was raised in a trade union household. My mother was a lifelong member of the International Ladies' Garment Workers' Union, the famed ILGWU. My heart generally always lies with the working man. It's hard for many people to look at a baseball player as a working man, since, after all, all that he's doing is playing a game, and the average major league player now makes more than $2 million a year. It is safe to say most people could live on that. The baseball players' union is also probably the strongest union in America. It has held together. It was first led ably by the brilliant Marvin Miller, who belongs in the Baseball Hall of Fame, and Donald Fehr, its current head and a student of Miller's philosophy. While Fehr doesn't have Marvin's personality, he is nevertheless a fighter for the people he represents.

The owners, on the other hand, are in a quandary. They have been given antitrust exemption by the United States Supreme Court. They have been an entertainment and a business. They can depreciate players the way other companies can depreciate furniture. While many teams are in financial straits, every time a team is sold, the seller makes a fortune. Somebody's making a fortune.

Other leagues have salary caps, with the top and the floor literally making the players partners of a sort. Ted Turner once called it a classic example of socialism at work. Baseball has no such system. Any baseball player can make anything. So the owners, attempting to put a control on their own spending at the top, want the players to give back rights that they have gained. I've never heard of any union doing that. Nevertheless, the players have to give something. President Bush, himself a former owner, should consider becoming directly involved. Not that baseball comes under the head of national security, but it is the national pastime, and it has been played through every war. It is important to the psyche of the public.

Since I know the President is a rabid fan, he could certainly help by putting the power of his office into labor negotiations. SANITY MUST PREVAIL. Baseball should have a floor, that is, no team should be allowed to have a payroll under $70 million, and payrolls over $90 million should be required to pay some sort of tax that would be spread among the poorest teams. The teams with the most money (Yankees, Mets, Dodgers) could help the teams with less money (Brewers, Royals, Pirates). This current situation could be a classic example of killing the goose that is laying the golden egg. If baseball has a work stoppage at any time, I doubt if the sport could truly recover. Some people think otherwise. They think the game could shut down, have long bargaining sessions, come to a long-term agreement, then start up again with giveaways and low prices and the like. I don't share that view.

When I was planning this book there was a real possibility that baseball would strike in 2002. Certainly, it was great news and a tremendous relief when it was announced that the players and owners had agreed to a new four-year contract, averting a strike at the last minute. I think on balance the fans came out ahead—as long as the teams in the smaller markets receiving the most dollars spend it on improving their team rather than padding their own coffers. If it all works out, the players will still be paid handsomely and the Kansas Cities and Pittsburghs should improve considerably.

I really think the fans brought the settlement about. Everyone I've talked to in the game tells me that the pressure from fans was enormous—something they had not seen or realized. So at least for four years, the cry of 'play ball!' will be heard throughout the land. For me, those two words are a beautiful part of the language and of the American fabric. Someone once said if you want to know what America's all about, look at baseball. That someone was right.

CHAPTER

9

ALL STAR

Baseball has brought me so many incredible moments with extraordinary people that will live forever in my heart and mind.

It was the 2000 World Series, the Mets against the Yankees in the famous Subway Series starring the longtime New York rivals. The Yankees would win in five. The first two games were played in Yankee Stadium. My friends Sid Young and Asher Dann, and my brother Marty and I, all went to the second game.

Fortunately I had been invited to the game by Mayor Rudy Giuliani. I sat next to him throughout the game won by the Yankees that night. That was the evening, by the way, in which Mike Piazza broke a bat at the plate and Roger Clemens, the Yankee pitcher, threw a piece of the bat at Piazza as he ran toward first. One of baseball's more dramatic moments, and I was sitting so close to it I could pick up the splinters.

The trip to the game is what makes the story memorable. My brother and I rode in the Mayor's car. The car behind us was a limousine company sedan in which Sid and Asher rode. The limousine driver had been told to stay right behind our car as we left the Regency Hotel at 61st and Park in Manhattan to head for Yankee Stadium in the Bronx. On the best day, this is a half-hour trip. With loads of rush-hour traffic and a World Series game, it's more like an hour. We made it in eleven minutes. We hit the siren and took off like the Taliban was in Queens. Siren blaring, I could see Sid and Asher in the back seat of the other car with their seat belts on, their car bobbing in and out but staying right behind us. There was a light drizzle falling. The roads were terribly crowded, but we were in the Mayor's car and we had a siren, and the car behind us was in our entourage of two. We gunned forward, we cut people off, we went right lane, center lane, left lane, we got off the exit and were quickly waved into the ballpark. We were up in George Steinbrenner's suite so fast that we never even turned our tickets in. No one ever ripped them in half, so technically, ours was an unrecorded attendance figure.

We were literally out of breath from a car ride. It was harrowing, but it was something to remember. Times like that—sitting in the owner's luxury box, munching goodies and soft drinks, spending time with Mike Wallace, Tom Cruise, Walter Cronkite, and various baseball dignitaries—still produce in me, the little Jewish kid from Brooklyn, the kind of thrill I could never have imagined while growing up rooting for the home team. I was sitting next to the Mayor for the entire game, chewing the special wheat flax or whatever it is prostate cancer victims eat—it's not bad, by the way. I was rooting in my heart for the Mets while Giuliani, an insane Yankee fan, went out of his mind on every pitch. . . .

This brings up another point. Why do otherwise normal, rational people go nuts about baseball? Everyone knows how Steinbrenner reacts when his team loses. Conversely, I truly believe the happiest moment in my friend Edward Bennett Williams' life, and one of the happiest in mine, was that day the Orioles won the 1983 World Series.

Ed was a fanatic too. The public never saw it, but those close to him knew it. How much of a fanatic? That same year the Orioles clinched the pennant on a Thursday, they were slated to face the White Sox the following Tuesday to see who would go to the World Series. Meanwhile, the Orioles had a meaningless three-game series at home with the Detroit Tigers. They had already clinched the pennant, so remember, this game means absolutely nothing. I was sitting next to Mr. Williams in his box behind home plate. The Tigers batter steps to the plate. The Orioles pitcher throws the first pitch of the game. The umpire says, Ball One and Edward Bennett Williams jumps up and yells, "FUCK!" I looked at him and said, "What the hell are you mad at?" He said, "We're going to get lethargic!

We're not going to concentrate! We're gonna lose here and then we're gonna lose next week!" I said, "Ed, you are a great trial attorney. You have so much knowledge, you may be the brightest person I know." As I'm saying this the second pitch is Ball Two. Now he screams louder, "See what I mean? This is doom." I said, "Ed, you are truly sick."

So many great baseball memories. One of the biggest thrills I ever had was when I went to an All-Star game in Baltimore and in the clubhouse before the game the Major League All-Stars were asking for *my* autograph. On baseballs. I still pinch myself over that. In fact, let's face it, if I could have been a baseball player I'd chuck the whole broadcasting career. I don't want to be great . . . I would have just liked to have hit .280. Played fifteen years, second base . . . maybe broadcast games after my playing career was over. That's not asking too much, is it? Right now I'd give it all up to be Commissioner. Why not? Nobody sits in front of you.

I remember the first time I met Stan Musial. I was sitting at Joe's Stone Crab restaurant in Miami Beach when someone tapped me on the shoulder and said, "I've seen you on television and I'd like to meet you." I turned around and it was Musial. I thought I'd die.

My brother, the lifelong Cardinals fan, was given a surprise birthday party by his wife on his sixtieth birthday. He didn't know where they were going. She flew him to St. Louis. They went to Bob Costas's house for dinner, went to the Cardinal game where he mingled in the clubhouse and on the field with the players, and at a dinner the next night was surprised by his seating companion, Stan Musial. He has never, ever forgotten that moment. You never do.

Even superstars in other professional sports are infected by a love of the game. I remember Joe Namath, the great football star, telling me once that if he could have been a major league baseball player he would much rather have played that game. Apparently he was quite a shortstop and pitcher, and he was scouted in his college days at Alabama. But the scouts generally agreed that his top level of play would have been Triple-A ball. Joe knew he could go farther in pro football, and selected it wisely. However, he told me, "If I could have played major league baseball, there's no comparison. The life is 100 times better. You last longer. You get to visit a city for three or four days, not run in and run out. You don't get hurt nearly as much or as badly. And you get to play offense and defense, which of course you don't get to do in football."

Bobby Knight, the great basketball coach, is a crazed baseball fan. A fanatical rooter for the Cardinals as well, Knight goes out of his way to attend any baseball game in any town he finds himself in. He has more friends in baseball than in basketball. He told me once,

"Baseball is definitely the most scientific and difficult of all the sports to play. The more you see it, the more you learn." I agree one-hundred percent.

How joyful is baseball? Tommy Lasorda, the former manager of the Dodgers, now in the Hall of Fame, told me that the biggest thrill of his life was to manage a winning team at a major league baseball game. His second-greatest thrill was to manage a losing game. Now that, dear friends, is love.

There were only sixteen teams in all of baseball when I was a kid. Now there are double that. But, basically, the game hasn't changed since its invention. It's a ball and a bat and some gloves. It's a Friday night or a Saturday afternoon ritual. It's the home white and the visiting grays.

The procedures that take place before a game are the same as years ago, with added calisthenics. They didn't do calisthenics a long time ago. Players make enough money now to report in shape, rather than to use the spring to get in shape.

Some things don't change. Every kid I know still loves to play baseball, and wants to master it, which is good, albeit impossible. Baseball stats are still the only ones that really matter.

I've been a fan for more than sixty years and still see things at a game that I've never seen before. Despite all of its headaches and self-imposed woes it remains the classic sport. So football and hockey and basketball, while all interesting and all commanding some of my attention, are really just taking up time while I wait for baseball to start again.

As in life, hope springs eternal. Youth will win out. "Wait till next year." "Hit one for me, Babe." PLAY BALL!

Once there were these two old friends who loved baseball. They were not unlike my boyhood friend Herb Cohen and myself. They spent many a year rooting for their teams, watching games together, traveling to World Series together, arguing, betting, and enjoying all the intricacies of the game.

One day one of the buddies, let's call him Herbie, broke the news that he was terminally ill and would die very soon. Naturally his best friend was devastated. Trying to buoy his ailing friend's spirits, his friend said "You know what I've always wondered? Is there baseball in heaven?" Herbie told him that if there was, and he could find a way to communicate with him, he'd do his best to let him know.

Sadly, Herbie died just a few weeks later.

One month to the day after Herbie died his friend's phone rang. When he picked it up there was Herbie's familiar voice on the other end telling him he had good news and bad news. The good news, Herbie said, was that yes indeed, there is baseball in heaven.

The friend was so thrilled to hear Herbie's voice again and to learn that there was actually baseball in heaven. "That's great, Herbie! What could the bad news be?"

"You're pitching Saturday."

I, for one, believe it wouldn't be heaven without baseball.